# JAGGED ROCKS OF
# WISDOM—NEGOTIATION

# OTHER BOOKS

## ALSO BY MORTEN LUND

*Jagged Rocks of Wisdom: Professional Advice for the New Attorney*

*Jagged Rocks of Wisdom—The Memo: Mastering the Legal Memorandum*

*Jagged Rocks of Wisdom—Contracts: Mastering the Science of Contract Drafting (forthcoming)*

## FOR THE LAW STUDENT

*The Art of the Law School Transfer: A Guide to Transferring Law Schools*

*Later-in-Life Lawyers: Tips for the Non-Traditional Law Student*

*Law School Fast Track: Essential Habits for Law School Success*

*Law School: Getting In, Getting Good, Getting the Gold*

*Law School Undercover: A Veteran Law Professor Tells the Truth About Admissions, Classes, Cases, Exams, Law Review, and More*

*Planet Law School II: What You Need to Know (Before You Go)— but Didn't Know to Ask…and No One Else Will Tell You*

*The Slacker's Guide to Law School: Success Without Stress*

## FOR THE SUMMER AND NEW ASSOCIATE

*The Insider's Guide to Getting a Big Firm Job: What Every Law Student Should Know About Interviewing*

*The Young Lawyer's Jungle Book: A Survival Guide*

## NON-LAW ADVENTURES

*College Fast Track: Essential Habits for Less Stress and More Success in College*

*Grains of Golden Sand: Adventures in War-Torn Africa*

*Training Wheels for Student Leaders: A Junior Counseling Program in Action*

# Jagged Rocks of Wisdom—Negotiation

## Mastering the Art of the Deal

### Morten Lund

The Fine Print Press

Honolulu

Copyright © 2011 by Morten Lund

Published by
The Fine Print Press, Ltd.
Honolulu, Hawaii
Website: www.fineprintpress.com
Email: info@fineprintpress.com


Library of Congress Cataloging-in-Publication Data

Lund, Morten, Lawyer.
    Jagged Rocks of Wisdom—Negotiation: Mastering the Art of the Deal / Morten Lund.
      p. cm.
    ISBN–13: 978-1-888960-09-9 (softcover : alk. paper)
    ISBN–10: 1-888960-09-4 (softcover : alk. paper)

    1. Practice of law—United States.   2. Negotiation in business—United States. I. Title.
KF300.L86 2011
302.3—dc22

                              2011006105




Cover design and typesetting by Designwoerks, Wichita, Kansas.
Editing by Chad Pickering and Thane Messinger.

The text face is Esprit Book, designed by Jovica Veljoviç and issued by ITC in 1985; supplemented with chapter headings in Castellar, designed by John Peters and issued by Monotype in 1957, section headings in Poppl-Laudatio, designed in 1982 by Friedrich Poppl for the H. Berthold AG Typefoundry of Berlin, and accent uses of American Typewriter, Helvetica Neue, and Law & Order.

PRINTED IN THE UNITED STATES OF AMERICA
20 19 18 17 16 15 14 13 12 11    10 9 8 7 6 5 4 3 2 1

# CONTENTS

# FOREWORD

Morten Lund has done it again.

In his first book, *Jagged Rocks of Wisdom: Professional Advice for the New Attorney,* Lund offers direct access to the secret world of the law partner's mind. It is a look that is enlightening, empowering, and, for those entering a professional practice, more than a little frightening.

In his second book, *Jagged Rocks of Wisdom—The Memo: Mastering the Legal Memorandum,* Lund tackles an essential skill of lawyering. A task much-feared and not always mastered, this is among the key proficiencies that will determine whether one will continue as a practicing attorney, or not.

In this, his third book, Lund broadens his considerable talents to an issue of importance to all professionals, extending far beyond mere law practice. This is the art and science of negotiation, as filtered through "21 Rules" for the professional negotiator.

It's no exaggeration to state that of every professional—whether in law, business, public affairs, you name it—all are expected to achieve goals for clients and for their organizations. These expectations underlie every aspect of their daily work. In a word, they must *negotiate.* Whether they see it, or accept it, negotiation—communicating with another to achieve a goal—is part of all professional work. Indeed, it is probably *the* part of professional work, in one way or another. (And, *psst,* it's the fun part.)

Negotiation is, however, a skill akin to learning to ride a bicycle. Daunting at first, nearly everyone seems to get the hang of it. More or less. The truth is that if one wants to be *good* at negotiation (or cycling), something more than just staying upright is required. Nearly anyone can get on a two-wheeled vehicle and go from Point A to Point B. Nearly anyone can walk into a room and "negotiate."

*Skill* at either of these—avoiding the potholes and cars, or achieving more than the other side is already prepared to give— requires both practice and insight. For most, being a so-so negotiator (or cyclist) is the unstated and unfortunate reality. For the fair-weather cyclist, this is hardly a major concern. For a professional negotiator, however, it is. After all, most potholes won't sink you, and most cars will swerve, because they are probably not out to get you.

Most opponents, however, *are* out to get you. Maybe not directly, but direct enough. Maybe not intentionally, but intentional enough.

Most professionals violate these 21 Rules all the time. I do. The difference is the extent to which the rules are known, and broken with fair reason. Dealing with a long-term counterpart is a very different beast than forging a new relationship. Unless one is prepared to bridge that difference, as the situation calls for it, even a polished veteran suddenly becomes the clumsy, rank amateur. Moreover, this is at base what Lund is getting at in his Rules: decide right or decide left, but *decide*. And decide with real knowledge and foresight.

* * *

Most negotiations are relatively sloppy affairs, and most negotiators accomplish their goals (or not) based as much on luck and circumstance as on any real skill. Indeed, to even speak of a "negotiator," one should contemplate a range of characters, from meek, decidedly nervous amateurs to skilled professionals to polished veterans to shuttle-diplomacy-scarred diplomats. Notably, it is the negotiator at the amateur side of the scale—which encompasses the bulk of those pressed into actual negotiation—who needs Lund's help the most. Sadly, few get much meaningful help in how, exactly, to approach negotiation.

In his 21 Rules, Lund aims to change this. He offers a clarity to the practice of negotiation that is as refreshing as it is unique. The concision might well be due to Lund's background as a partner in a fast-paced law practice, where theorizing and philosophizing, while a part of law practice to be sure, must be tied to concrete and specific goals for very real and very cost-conscious clients. Anything less is both distracting and hugely wasteful, and thus unacceptable. This is a world in which the word *unacceptable* means what it says.

The clarity is more remarkable still. Lund's 21 Rules distill points and usable approaches from a shadowy vapor of *ad hoc* tactics used time and again, with predictably uneven results. Lund's advice will settle much of that fog, revealing practical, comprehensible tips. The concision and clarity of Lund's 21 Rules are a result of a real-world, real-consequences approach: negotiation is not abstract.

Prussian General von Moltke's dictum that a battle plan never survives its first contact with the enemy has become cliché, even if we don't always act upon this truth. So too with negotiation. "Preparing" in an abstract way—such as in assuming the standard, interest-based negotiation stance that looks beyond the opponent's "mere" stated positions—can quickly be made pointless as the opening discussions reveal that positional bargaining is *their* approach, period. It takes two to tango. And it takes both to be interested in slow-dancing.

Paradoxically, while looking past rules to the essential nature of war (in contrast with many of his contemporaries), von Moltke focused on extensive preparation for an array of potential outcomes, rather than on a set-piece sequence of static battle plans. Thus his dictum…and thus the parallel to our topic, negotiation. Lund's focus on this essential nature of negotiation is exactly right.

As Lund states at several points, negotiation should not be a "battle" in the sense above—but it can be. Thus, the wise negotiator is prepared. And this preparation takes the form of each of these 21 Rules. One could list each, and realize immediately its applicability and importance: Lund's 21 Rules are a concrete, discrete, achievable set of directives to meet the immediate objectives, and to better place the negotiator for victory. If well done, such victory should be mutual—but as Lund also states, that is an incidental benefit, not a goal in itself.

\* \* \*

As I sat down to read the manuscript for this book, I honestly didn't have much by way of expectations for it—not because of the author, but because of the subject. I know and respect Lund and his work, and my own work in negotiation is from a rather different angle. Yet as I started, it became immediately obvious just how unique and powerful Lund's advice is. This is exactly what the new professional should know about this crucially important part of office life—and indeed of all of life. More than that, this is what *everyone* should think about when attempting to interact with another person for some gain, advantage, or accolade. It doesn't matter what.

The second aspect that impressed me about this book was an almost magical combination of *panache* to go with the actual Rules. His use of words—"un-goals," "cliffs," "Weasel-hunting"— add an element of delight to an otherwise dry subject. Negotiation is *not* dry; neither should a book about it be. Negotiation involves two stories (at least)—often in conflict, and nearly always with varying shades of truth and appearance. When the sides meet, most bets are off. This is *exciting* stuff...and Lund makes it so.

His use of language is at times sublime. With tongue firmly in cheek, he tells us to "Sit Down and Shut Up." When's the last time you wanted to say that? And how many times have you known, in your heart of hearts, that you deserved to be told that?

He challenges us with "Only the Weak Do Not Care," then taunts us with "Be A Hardass," and then a bit of jujitsu with "Sometimes It *Is* About You."

This is not your run-of-the-mill book on negotiating.

Among Lund's admonishments are constellations of advice/nagging. Clearly we all know we're *supposed* to prepare, and just as clearly we know that we almost never prepare as much as we should. Sometimes we prepare not at all. We wing it, supposing our brilliance and upstanding character will win the day. And besides, there just aren't enough hours in the day and who's really going to notice. Well, for starters, the other side will.

As good as these Rules are, when we look past them we see the core concern: these constellations coalesce around a set of oft-violated yet rock-solid best practices. Numerous of Lund's rules concern a single commandment: *Thou shalt prepare.*

*Preparation* means everything Lund writes in Rule #1 ("What Are You Trying To Achieve?") and Rule #2 ("What Are *They* Trying To Achieve?") and obviously Rule #3 ("Prepare; Then Prepare Some More") and less obviously Rule #4 ("It's All About Credibility") and Rule #11 ("Understand The Environment") and Rule #12 ("Control The Environment") and Rule #13 ("Understand The People—Including Yourself") and Rule #20 ("Think Sideways")…and good chunks of the remaining rules. Preparation counts.

A second, not-too-distant constellation is all about *credibility*. This draws in Rule #4 ("It's All About Credibility") and Rule #5 ("Take The High Road") and still more with Rule #9 ("Bring Credibility To The Table") and Rule #13 ("Understand The People—Including Yourself") and Rule #14 ("Be Alpha"), and even Rules #16 ("Logic Is Your Friend") and #19 (Watch The Tide"). Credibility counts.

Still another constellation is found in the "real stuff"—those Rules relating to what a negotiator is supposed to *do* in a live negotiation. The truth, as Lund states, is that while this is what we see, and what we think of and focus on, in many ways this is the anticlimax of the real world of negotiation—or at least a sideshow. The best negotiator wins because of what happens before everyone walks into the room.

Still, if anything Lund is all the greater in these areas. His take on what to actually do as a negotiator is nothing short of magnificent. He flips the world of power politics upside down in Rule #7 ("Master The Art of Appeasement"). In a novel and remarkable Rule, he overturns seven decades of assumptions about the use of power *and* provides negotiators a potent tool. Moreover, his simple, reasonable definition makes the testing of his advice readily accomplished, and as a bonus overturns much diplomatic nicety. If this doesn't cause an uproar among historians and other professional trouble-handlers, perhaps nothing will.

Likewise, in Rule #8 ("... And Also The Salami"), Lund validates Rule #7 by offering its opposite. So, whether attacking or defending, the negotiator has comprehensible ways to maneuver— or fight.

In Rule #17 ("Nail Down The Weasel") he offers realistic ways to combat bad behavior in negotiation, surely one of the reasons negotiators fail. And in Rule #18 ("Give And Take...Or Not"), he avoids the saccharine emptiness that animates many negotiators who are either too stern or too willowy, often in the wrong ways at the wrong times.

Tying together all of the above are connecting themes, such as in Rule #10 ("Care"), Rule #16 ("Logic Is Your Friend"), and Rule #19 ("Watch The Tide").

It's impressive to read so much useful wisdom in such a relatively compact book. And throughout, some phrases are just too cool for paraphrasing:

"Appear Reasonable."

"Rules, Schmules?"

"Practice Makes Less Stupid."

"Know What You Don't Know."

"Dance the Weasel Dance."

"Identify Your Cliffs."

"Winning every argument is not your goal. Achieving your goals—*that* is your goal."

"Never throw a teammate to the sharks. He will drag you down with him."

"Sometimes It *Is* About You."

Indeed so. And doesn't this make for rather more interesting reading—and more useful advice—than abstract musings on abstract adversaries? This is the beauty of Lund's work.

\* \* \*

Morten Lund offers the negotiator a concise, powerful companion. One danger in negotiation is an immodest bravado—or a falsely innocent view of the world. Unfortunately, both views are too often on display in conference rooms the nation over. Reading these Rules, as conflicting as they sometimes are, will serve as an antidote to either perilous extreme.

*Negotiation* is itself a precarious word, as it implies too much, and covers far too many possibilities. Therein lies the trap for the unwary negotiator, and therein lies the beauty of Lund's book.

You would be extraordinarily lucky to have a mentor such as he at your side. With this book, your silent mentor is with you, standing watch as you embark on your many negotiation voyages.

Best of luck to you in your travels.

Thane J. Messinger

*Law School: Getting In, Getting Good, Getting the Gold*

*The Young Lawyer's Jungle Book: A Survival Guide*

Spring 2011

# INTRODUCTION

I am a professional negotiator.

As an attorney I perform many tasks, but one of the most important roles I play is that of a negotiator. This role has several aspects and variations: Sometimes I negotiate in person, sometimes on paper, while other times I advise clients on their negotiations without my direct participation. Sometimes I simply draft the documents preceding or resulting from the direct negotiations. Regardless of the mechanics, a defining feature of my professional existence is negotiation. One way or another, I help my clients achieve their goals—if necessary at the expense of others.

If you are a non-attorney reader who just realized that you are reading a book for lawyers, fear not: Most, if not all, of this book is just as applicable to non-lawyer negotiators. While lawyers are negotiators as part of their professional role, so too are professionals in business, public service, non-profits—everywhere. Negotiation is a part of life. The question is not whether one is a negotiator. The question is whether one is a good negotiator—or, more specifically, a whether one is a good negotiator on purpose.

We might also think of being a good negotiator *by design,* meaning that you craft a plan and take specific steps toward that plan. To this end I offer a number of specific suggestions for making your approach to negotiation more deliberate. It may appear that some of the suggestions are extreme—and indeed they are extreme, at least for some circumstances. If you fully and literally applied every recommendation in this book to every telephone call, you would spend weeks preparing for every six-minute exchange, and you would spend as much mental effort planning social chit-chat as planning your actual deal. That may be appropriate for some telephone calls, but most of the time this approach would render you useless. Instead, it is my hope that context-appropriate implementation of my Rules will become second nature, so that little extra time is needed.

It would be bizarre (and probably impossible) to apply every strategy and tactic in full to every negotiation. You must decide at each step what will work and what will not. No two situations are the same, and you must make the call—but make the call, and do so with deliberate intent.

I have not studied negotiation in a formal setting. I learned the hard way: watching and imitating; trial and error. This is the way most negotiators learn the trade. Some may have attended a seminar or workshop, some might even have taken a negotiation course in school, but overwhelmingly we learn by doing. While this obviously works, it is also wasteful. Sink or swim is wasteful. If we want our new negotiators to negotiate well we ought to tell you how, not just wait for you to figure it out—or not.

This book is an effort to pass on my own hard-earned learning, accumulated over the course of many years. This book is not a scholarly treatise—it is a guidebook based on personal experience. Negotiation is at its core two (or more) people exchanging ideas and trying to come to agreement on something of some importance to them. Ultimately negotiations are social interactions. As a result, a deep understanding of how to interact with others is the key to being a good negotiator, and indeed that is the central theme of this book.

As in the two prior *Jagged Rocks of Wisdom* books, there are anecdotes scattered throughout this book for your information and amusement. These anecdotes describe actual events. While details may have been changed to protect the innocent and the not-so-innocent (not to mention client confidences), each story happened more or less exactly as described. You should read these with great care, for they are living proof that even the seemingly obvious is frequently missed. An important caveat, however: Some anecdotes were selected in part for their colorful and dramatic exchanges. Do not extrapolate from this that you should always be confrontational or rude. Apply the Rule, not the anecdote.

In addition to the anecdotes you will find occasional "Pro Tips"—suggestions for specific techniques to try, or observations for contemplation. You will find some helpful and others goofy. Do not let the Pro Tips distract you from the underlying principles. Apply the Rule, not the Pro Tip.

The terminology I use is my own—I suspect you will face blank stares (at best) if you talk to your colleagues or professors about "un-goals" or "doing the Salami." The terms are partly my own invention for writing convenience, and partly slang I have come across over the years. Use or modify them as you will.

Which leads to a caution on the term "opponent." I use "opponent" throughout this book to describe the "other side" in the negotiation. Quite often, however, your opponent is not an adversary in any real-life sense. To the contrary, your opponents will frequently be your clients' business partners, and negotiations can be very friendly indeed. "Opponent" need not mean "hostile."

Everything described in this book works both ways. Don't commit errors; spot them in others. Use the strategies; defend against those same strategies. Some of this reciprocal bilateralism is described for certain Rules, but mostly it is left to you to extrapolate and apply. Just imagine that your opponent has also read this book, and you are being evaluated even as you are evaluating her. As the first two Rules illustrate, you must consider everything from both sides—including the Rules themselves.

Many of the Rules in this book will at times appear to conflict with other Rules, and the logic of a Rule might even seem internally inconsistent. This is the nature of reality, and it is your job to find the best way to reconcile those differences and find the true path—*your* true path.

Good luck.

# Note to the Negotiator

This book was written with a lawyer audience in mind. The Rules I describe are, however, of broad application to all negotiators, and will be just as useful to non-lawyers as to lawyers—perhaps even more so.

Clients, for example, are a large part of the success (or failure) of any negotiation. How well (or poorly) a client and attorney confer and interact determine to a large degree the outcome of any particular negotiation. It thus makes sense for both to understand the rules of the game—and the Rules of that negotiation, as each should understand them. Moreover, a client who understands the role and strategies of the lawyer can make the lawyer more effective.

There's yet another group for whom these Rules are useful: *non*-clients. Adding an attorney to a negotiation—nearly any negotiation—is adding a powerful negotiating lever. You will see how many of these Rules can be made more effective when someone else is applying them on your behalf. Conversely, going into a negotiation alone (as we all do, in a variety of situations) makes the outcome even more dependent upon our individual skill. "Alone" need not equal "weak."

There's still another category: Where the "client" is not a simple principal. In such spaces, as with a government agency or large organization, there *is* a client—but there is so much more. The Rules of negotiation grow in interrelated complexity, and thus take on added importance in business as well as government, far beyond mere law.

These Rules are thus well worth pondering—before, during, and after the actual negotiation—whether as an attorney, client, executive, official, employee, or political scientist.

# LESSONS FROM PRIOR BOOKS

Unlike the other books in the *Jagged Rocks of Wisdom* series, this book makes little mention of written perfection, and no mention of reading bosses' minds or of office politics. Indeed, there is precious little nitpicky or "lawyerly" stuff in this book at all—in part because negotiation involves psychology, economics, raw power…many things in addition to law (or any other field). Perhaps most importantly, unlike the other books, this book is not (directly) about pleasing a law partner or other boss, but about your own improvement.

Despite these differences, however, there are important lessons to be drawn from the other *Jagged Rocks of Wisdom* books, and some of those lessons are worth mentioning again here. In particular, I encourage you to remember these important jagged rocks:

## PROOFREAD

Yes, proofread. This may be the only book I will ever write without a chapter about proofreading, but proofreading remains relevant and important here as well. Did you read the part in the introduction about how some negotiations are in writing? And where there is writing, there is proofreading. An improperly spelled argument is not only not a convincing argument, it is one that is weakened, sometimes fatally so, for all the reasons spelled out in the Rules—such as those concerning your credibility.

## BE SOCIALLY AWARE

Perhaps no part of the legal profession requires greater social facility than negotiation. Negotiation is ultimately a social exercise, and if you are not aware of your social surroundings you will not succeed. The key word is *aware*. The social cues are there, if you only pay attention. If you are forever applying the wrong social conventions because you weren't paying attention, it matters not that your intentions were good. The damage is just as real. Most of the Rules in this book are discussions of the social interactions inherent in and to negotiations. Take the hint and act accordingly.

## UNDERSTAND THE FACTS...INCLUDING THE ONES YOU DON'T KNOW

You will read much in the Rules about preparation. One of the most important aspects of this preparation is the full and complete understanding of the facts. Negotiations are fact-specific: they do not exist in a vacuum. Without facts all you have is an academic discussion. And while academic discussions are amusing, they are not negotiation. To be successful at any negotiation, you must fully comprehend the universe of facts relating to *that* negotiation.

## HAVE FUN

That's right, I said it—have fun. Negotiation is *fun*. It is perhaps my favorite part of the job. It is a game, a challenge, and a social exchange all rolled into one, with a giant dollop of ego-trip on top. Negotiations do not have to be unpleasantly adversarial—indeed they should not be if it can be avoided. If your negotiations frequently descend into unpleasant bickering, you are probably doing it wrong.

# THE RULES

# Rule Number 1

# What Are You Trying To Achieve?

This Rule lays the foundation for everything that follows. It is the most important Rule in the entire book. Read this Rule carefully, but do not leave it behind after doing so. This Rule should be in your mind as you read the rest of the book, and always in your mind as you engage in actual negotiations. This Rule should be the central motivating force throughout the entire process.

## IDENTIFY YOUR GOALS

Rule #1 is simply the title question itself: What are you trying to achieve?

*Exactly* what are you trying to achieve?

Answer the question for yourself. But be specific…be very specific. This sounds like an easy task, and sometimes it is—but often it is not. If it were always easy, this Rule would not be ignored constantly. And no, this did not suddenly become a motivational self-help book. This Rule is a central negotiation strategy. It is *the* central negotiation strategy. You *must* identify your goals.

Imagine that you are unhappy with the service you received at a hotel during a recent vacation. So you call the hotel manager to complain. Upon hearing your grievances, the manager expresses sympathy, and then asks "What would like us to do?" And you have no idea what to say, because frankly you had not thought about what you wanted. You just knew you were upset. Are you looking for an apology? A refund? A free meal at your next visit? If you have not thought about it *before* you call to complain, you will accomplish little, and will essentially be forced to accept whatever offer is made. With some preparation, however, you would have been able to take charge of the exchange and achieve a better result.

The same applies when "negotiating" in social situations. Imagine yourself at a cocktail party, and a social rival is discussing politics—he is explaining to his adoring crowd why Congress should quickly legalize marijuana. As it turns out, marijuana policy is something you know well (and disagree with him about). You leap into the fray.

Stop!

First, ask yourself: What are you trying to achieve?

If you do not ask yourself this question, you will inadvertently and inevitably fail at one or more of your goals. So: Are you trying to convince fellow citizens and voters that marijuana is bad and should remain illegal? Or are you trying to humiliate this jerk? Or are you trying to convince him that you are cool and smart and you should be friends? Or are you trying to impress the crowd? Or a certain someone in the crowd?

None of these goals are right—or wrong. It is up to you to know whether you want to "win" the debate, or instead just want people to like you. The point is that each goal almost certainly requires a different approach. You might be able to accomplish some of those goals, but not all. You must choose. If you do not, you are acting without purpose, and the outcome may not be to your liking. Then, later, after you have delivered the final crushing blow to your opponent's arguments and victory is yours, you look around and realize that nobody wants to talk to you and you wonder why. Clearly you did not think your cunning plan all the way through. You didn't keep your goal in sight. How could you, when you didn't even identify your goal to begin with? Pick any goal you want—I don't care. But *pick one.*

Your goals may not be what you think they are. At a minimum, they are almost always more complex and layered than you think, and simply identifying "the goal" is insufficient. There will almost never be just a single goal.

Are you negotiating to buy a car? Then you want to achieve buying a car. You also want to achieve not paying more than $35,000, including the upgraded stereo and leather seats. That's the easy part. But you are not done, for this is not all that you want to achieve.

In addition to the car, the stereo, and the leather seats, you also want a pleasant experience. Perhaps you want to establish a relationship with the dealer to ensure good service for your car, and to smooth the way for the next car purchase. And you also want to feel good about the purchase—you don't want to feel as if you got ripped off. You don't want your wife/husband/co-workers to think you made a bad deal. You don't want to be embarrassed about what you paid. You want to minimize "buyer's regret."

---

A friend asked for my assistance with a letter he was writing to a local newspaper. He was very unhappy with the treatment he had received in a recent article, and he was writing to the paper to correct the facts and give them a piece of his mind.

The letter was well written, and did in fact give the newspaper a piece of his mind. What it did not do, however, was state any demand for anything at all—not even a correction or retraction.

I asked my friend what he wanted to achieve with the letter. What I got in return was a blank stare.

---

The layers of what you want can go on and on. Sometimes the goals are obvious, sometimes subtle, and they usually interact. You do not have to clearly identify each and every goal—but you must know what your main purposes are, and understand the limitations that you are placing on yourself with those goals.

So—what are you trying to achieve? What are you *really* trying to achieve? If you don't know, how can you possibly achieve it?

## IDENTIFY YOUR UN-GOALS

Identifying your goals, however, is not enough. Once you have identified your goals and know what you are trying to achieve, you must also ask and answer the immediate corollary question: What are you *not* trying to achieve?

The evil twin of a goal is an "un-goal." Un-goals are fake "goals" that attract you like a moth to a flame, usually without you realizing that you are being self-destructive. Un-goals are things that you are not trying to achieve, or should not be trying to achieve, but that nevertheless tempt and motivate you.

For instance, when negotiating to buy a car, you are *not* trying to please or impress the car salesman. Don't waste your time or money trying. This is perhaps the single most common un-goal of all: the desire to please and impress. If you look, you will see it all around you, and you will catch yourself wanting to do it as well.

Don't.

Sometimes your actual goals include pleasing people—but your goals should not include pleasing *everyone,* let alone pleasing your opponent. This is a certain path to failure, and is a most definite un-goal in almost any circumstance.

---

We represented the borrower in a loan transaction, and we were negotiating a lender consent with our supplier—a requirement for the loan, but not a contract we would be party to.

We were struggling to find terms that would be reasonable to both the supplier and the lender, and negotiations had stalled. The partner on the deal pulled the client aside and reminded him that our goal was not to find optimal terms for either the supplier or the lender—our goal was to borrow money. Anything beyond what was minimally necessary to get the loan closed was not really our concern.

We returned to the conference call, and pushed through terms that may not have been great for either the lender or the supplier, but which were good enough to get the loan issued—which was what *we* wanted.

---

If you are buying a car, don't worry about what the car salesman thinks of you, unless this is one of your stated goals for some reason. Maybe he is your brother-in-law. But otherwise, if you see that the salesman appears to be getting sad/stressed/worried, *good!* Don't feel sorry for him. That is part of his job, and if he is not at least a little stressed, chances are it is *you* who is being taken advantage of. It is not your goal to make him happy. It is your goal to get a good car at a good price…with the upgraded stereo and leather seats. Focus on that. Don't be distracted by the un-goal.

Many people try to avoid tension and confrontation, and will make concessions just to be nice, or because their opponent is friendly, or just because it is easier than facing the problem. This is nothing more than succumbing to that same un-goal: wanting to please people.

Car salesmen, of course, understand this and take advantage of un-goals, as do skilled negotiators of all kinds. The charming sales-man with the thousand-watt grin can squeeze an extra few dollars out of the customer—or an extra few thousand dollars—because the customer can't help but wanting to please her new friend and avoid disappointing him. That salesman has his goals organized; the customer does not. He achieves his goals; the customer does not. Salesmen are masters of the un-goal. Learn from them.

Another common un-goal is ego-boosting. This un-goal is the simple desire to feel good, usually by establishing your superiority over others. This is the taunt, the brag, the gratuitous fist-pump. It is often displayed in sports and games of all kinds, but is unfortu-nately pervasive in the boardroom as well. It is also popular with attorneys and other professional negotiators, who often have Texas-sized egos to begin with and quite enjoy feeling good about themselves.

An illustration of this un-goal in action can be seen at the poker table, when a poor player makes an incorrect or foolish play. An intermediate player may mock the poor player or lecture him, in an attempt to boost his own ego by displaying knowledge of the game and belittling the beginner. The truly skilled player, on the other hand, will do no such thing. The skilled poker player will smile, perhaps apologize for her good luck, and encourage the poor player to stick around. The skilled player has her goal identified:

Win money. The intermediate player is getting distracted by the un-goal of ego-boosting. The intermediate player is so determined to impress everybody at the table with his skill and knowledge of the game that he chases away all the bad players with his unpleasant behavior. As a result, he is now left playing only with superior players, and will end up *losing* money. By being distracted by his un-goal, this player failed to achieve his real goal. More specifically, he had not organized his goals and un-goals to begin with, and was therefore unable to identify his own mistake.

Yet another common un-goal, and a subtly dangerous one, is the determination to defeat your opponent. Let me be very clear on this: Keeping your opponents from their goals is never your goal. Never. Your goal is to achieve your *own* goals. Your goals may be incompatible with your opponents' goals, but this does not make their prevention a goal of its own. If in the process of achieving your goals you preclude your opponents from achieving theirs, this is purely an incidental side effect. If anything, helping your opponents achieve their goals should be an intermediate goal of yours, as this will make them more inclined to help you with your goals. This is the subject matter of Rule #18 ("Give And Take...Or Not").

It is a common sight to see rookie negotiators expend vast effort at preventing their opponent from gaining a goal that would cost the rookie nothing to surrender. The rookie is stuck in "yield nothing" mode. This grand effort will gain him nothing, and will portray him as obnoxious and stubborn, which will cost him credibility and make him less effective at achieving his true goals. He has no concern for whether this point has any value, or how it relates to his goals—his only concern is to win Win WIN! He is negotiating for the rush, the excitement, the glory of victory. At the bar that night he will brag to his buddies about how he held the line on this issue or the other, and about how tough of a negotiator he is, all the while not realizing how ineffective and counterproductive he really was.

Don't do it. Winning every argument is not your goal. Achieving your goals—*that* is your goal.

Athletes around the world understand this principle. Hence what is perhaps the single most popular sports saying of all time: Keep your eye on the ball. Don't be distracted by the roaring crowd, the taunting catcher, or the fact that you have struck out five times in a row. Your goal is to hit the ball. That's it. Just hit the ball. So…keep your eye on the ball.

Un-goals come in many shapes and sizes, and you need to be constantly vigilant to ensure that you resist their siren song. That written, you will have noticed that the examples I have mentioned are social and emotional in nature. This is no coincidence. More often than not, it is emotion and social constraints that get in the way of achieving our true goals. While there can be "substantive" un-goals, it is the social and emotional un-goals that are most pervasive—and insidious.

For attorneys this is a double challenge, because we are (typically) not negotiating our own causes. There are times when emotional un-goals are actually goals (many people do play poker primarily for fun, ego-boosting, and other non-monetary reasons, for instance), but it will never be the case that the ego-boosting of the *attorney* is a goal for the client.

> **Pro Tip:** Be ready to be the fall-guy. Agreeing with your client to "blame the lawyer" for an unpopular position can help achieve your client's goals.

Your function as an attorney-negotiator is to achieve the *client's* goals, not your own. To accomplish this, you must first identify those goals, and then be wary of the lure of the un-goals— both the client's un-goals and your own.

## IDENTIFY YOUR CLIFFS

In addition to the things you are specifically trying to achieve (goals) and things you are not trying to achieve (un-goals), there will be things you are specifically trying to avoid. These "cliffs" are the true opposites of goals. Cliffs might be substantive issues where you cannot give, or they might be softer and social in nature, such as being embarrassed or losing credibility.

The substantive cliffs are usually fairly easy to spot and avoid ("don't sell the car below cost," or "don't agree to consequential damages"), but the social cliffs can be tricky and are the ones you need to worry about. Social cliffs are often a matter of degree. Maybe you aren't trying to impress the guys at the bar—but you don't want them to hate you either. You don't care about making the salesman happy—but you don't want to make him so mad that out of spite he kills the deal. When negotiating with your boss for a raise, you don't want to make him so angry that you get fired instead of promoted. Behavior that makes you look foolish is a cliff. Behavior that makes you look inattentive or ignorant is a cliff. Behavior that makes you look unreasonable or irrational is a cliff. Anything that decreases your credibility is a cliff.

> Whenever an associate asks me for advice about a course of action, regardless of the subject matter, my rote response is "What are you trying to achieve?"
>
> I am sure they find it quite annoying, but it is also quite effective.
>
> Due to the annoyance factor I try to be more subtle when talking with clients or my wife, but I still endeavor to focus the conversation on the underlying goals.

Cliffs can be as dangerous as un-goals. Like goals, they must be identified ahead of time. If you do not identify the goals you will probably not accomplish them; if you do not identify the cliffs you probably *will* accomplish those—and not realize it until too late.

Cliffs can force you into defeat. Looking like an incompetent fool or a total jerk is tantamount to losing the negotiation, since you will be unable to accomplish your goals. Being backed against a substantive issue where you cannot give forces you to choose between giving the un-givable and walking away from the deal entirely. This is perhaps the primary means by which negotiations are won and lost, particularly for beginning negotiators. Whether due to insufficient preparation or insufficient understanding, beginners find themselves in situations where they have no response, where they are stuttering and grasping at straws to explain their position, and where they eventually have no choice but agree to their opponent's demands, for to do otherwise would destroy any remaining shreds of professional credibility. Sometimes negotiation can simply be a race to push the opponent off a social cliff.

## THERE ARE GOALS AND THEN THERE ARE *GOALS*

Not all cliffs and goals are created equal. You have to not only identify the goals and cliffs, but also understand how they relate to each other. Some goals/cliffs are true "must haves" (or must avoids), but most are negotiable to some degree or another. It might be worth trading one goal for another—but only the correct goals. You must truly understand which goals are central to the purpose of the client, and which goals are merely desirable—the must-haves versus the nice-to-haves. You might compromise on a secondary goal, but a main goal is just that: main.

Some goals and cliffs are intermediaries—the only reason you want to avoid early termination of the contract is because the payment schedule is rear-heavy, and your main goal, your top-level goal, is "getting paid." This is important to understand because things change. If the payment schedule gets front-loaded, then the importance of the "avoid early termination" cliff is reduced, and it may no longer be a cliff at all. Be careful not to confuse goals (or cliffs) that are truly goals in their own right with goals that are mere intermediate goals—stepping-stones to other goals. Both are important, but achieving intermediate goals is not the point of the negotiation. Your top-level goals, your main goals, your central goals—those are the goals you have to keep your eye on.

An intermediate goal can easily become an un-goal if you do not pay attention.

It is essential that you get your top-level goals and cliffs straight before entering the discussion. Otherwise you might find yourself forgetting what you are trying to accomplish. A clever opponent can talk you right out of your central goal if you don't pay close attention and keep your eye on the ball. She will dazzle you with secondary goals and un-goals, and you won't even know she is picking your pocket until it is too late. A common attribute of the beginner negotiator is to apply excessive effort to minor issues while disregarding what is truly important. Don't do it.

**Pro Tip:** Make a point of occasionally revisiting your list of goals, to remind yourself of what is truly important.

Reality is fluid, and so must be your goals and your cliffs. You must identify changed circumstances that affect the existence and prioritization of your goals and cliffs, and adapt your positions accordingly. This goes both ways: You must be ready to devalue or abandon goals or cliffs as things change, but it is equally important that you identify goals and cliffs that increase in value due to changed circumstances, or entirely new goals or cliffs that suddenly appear.

Yes, you must determine what it is you are trying to achieve, but this task is never finished. Indeed it is not really a task at all, but a process—it is a mental approach that you must vigilantly apply at all times.

In short, your job is to work towards the goals and away from the cliffs, while pointedly ignoring the un-goals. Sounds basic? It is. Yet this basic principle is violated and ignored every day by amateurs and professionals alike. Don't let that be you. Identify

**Pro Tip:** If you find yourself getting angry, you might be succumbing to an un-goal.

what you are trying to achieve, what you are not trying to achieve, and what you are actively trying to avoid.

# Rule Number 2

# What Are *They* Trying To Achieve?

Once you have identified your goals, your un-goals, and your cliffs, you are halfway there. Now you must identify the goals, un-goals, and cliffs of your opponent.

Why is this important? Why should you care what your opponent wants? After all, didn't we just finish saying how the purpose of negotiation is for you to achieve *your* goals?

## It's Not All About You

Yes, the purpose of the negotiation is for you to achieve your goals. But there will come a time when you have to trade something to achieve your goals. Negotiation is a social exercise, and unless you understand your opponent's motivations as well as your own, you will not know which potential concession he values—or how much.

> Opposing counsel had sent me a markup of my contract with his comments and changes. He had made one particular change that was puzzling—it seemed oddly out-of-market and generally unjustified in the context of the transaction.
>
> I discussed this with my client, trying to ascertain what the other side was trying to achieve. The client suggested that we just strike the offending change and move on—and doing so would have been perfectly legitimate on our part.
>
> Opposing counsel was a sharp attorney, and would not have randomly made a change like this. So instead of simply striking the change—which might have led to additional frustrations on a side issue—I sought him out prior to the next session. Once I understood what he was trying to accomplish with the change, it made sense. We were able to reach an intelligent compromise, instead of wasting time with back-and-forth edits.

Your opponent will not simply agree to your goals because you ask nicely. Were it that easy you would not be negotiating. By definition you are at the negotiating table because your opponent is not willing to just give you what you want. Invariably, your opponent is holding your goals hostage because she wants something from you. And how can you determine whether to pay if you do not know the ransom? Therefore, you must first determine your opponent's goals before meaningful negotiations can even occur.

How do you determine your opponent's goals?

Start with this: Ask.

The other side usually wants you to know what their goals are—more or less, anyway—and if you just ask her what she wants, she is quite likely to tell you. She won't tell you her "super-secret bottom-line best price," but she will probably share with you most everything else.

Once this exchange has commenced, you will be able to explore your opponent's goals much like you have explored your own. There is a good chance your opponent does not fully understand her own goals. This is your chance to help. Drill down: If she says she must have delivery within 90 days, find out why. Most likely that deadline is driven by something else, and she doesn't really care about 90 days, just so long as her underlying need is met in some fashion. "90 days" is merely an intermediate goal, not her central goal. Help your opponent understand what she really wants, instead of what she thinks she wants.

Responding only to the stated goals of your opponent is a mistake. It is a mistake partly because she may not be truthful about what her goals are, but it is mostly a mistake because the stated goals are almost always the concrete implementation of the goals—intermediate goals—and your purpose should be to address your opponent's top-level goals. Getting distracted by your opponent's intermediate goals is a mistake.

Seek out the top-level goals—both your own and those of your opponent.

While asking your opponent about her goals is a good place to start, it is usually not enough to get to the bottom (or the top) of things. You have to be contemplative. You have to place yourself in your opponent's shoes, and view things from her perspective. This is not necessarily some sinister attempt at reading her mind, just an honest attempt at understanding her motivations. There is no great mystery here, and no real expertise or technique required. Mainly you just need to revisit the issues from the other side.

> **Pro Tip:** If your opponent is wrong about his own goals, you don't necessarily have to tell him. Sometimes it is better to just take note of what he really wants. For later.

It is easy to get so wrapped up in your own little universe of "our side" that you start behaving as if the "other side" is your mirror image, when in fact this is hardly ever so. Their goals will almost certainly not be just the opposite of yours. The world does not move along a single axis, and neither do the wants or needs of parties to a negotiation. Her goals will be *her* goals, not the reverse of your goals.

This process is ongoing. Perhaps even more than the list of your own goals, your list of your opponent's goals (and un-goals, and cliffs) will be fluid. As you gain information or the situation changes, you will need to be vigilant so as to not miss a shift in your opponent's motivations.

## MONEY DOES NOT MAKE THE WORLD GO AROUND

Of particular importance is understanding the value of money. Money is usually, in one form or other, at the center of business negotiations. This frequently leads beginning negotiators to reduce negotiations to nothing but dollars, and to evaluate goals and arguments purely in terms of cash value. If they have a game theory intro class under their

> **Pro Tip:** Separate the goals that can be met by throwing money at them from the goals that cannot.

belt, they may even translate dollars into "payoffs" (the currency of game theory). This reductionist approach is incorrect for at least three reasons.

First, this is the second Rule in the book discussing goals—and I am only on Rule #2. You should have noticed that there is nothing in either Rule saying that goals are all monetary. To the contrary, I have repeatedly pointed out various non-monetary goals. It is quite possible to meet all of your (or your opponent's) monetary goals while failing miserably at reaching a satisfactory deal. This mistake (quantifying all goals as monetary) is particularly easy to do with your opponent's goals. You are obviously closer to your own goals than your opponent's, and it is easy to disregard your opponent's "soft" goals. This is a mistake. Thinking of your opponent as an accounting decision-machine is incorrect. There are other goals in the calculus, and you must identify *all* goals, not just the ones represented by dollars.

Second, your opponent's decisions will be influenced by his un-goals as well as by his goals. Thinking of your opponent as a fully rational decision-machine is also incorrect. If your opponent is attached to his un-goals (which are often not monetary), failing to meet—or at least address—those un-goals will kill the deal as surely as failing to meet the central monetary goals.

> **Pro Tip:** When posing a hypothetical scenario, using irrelevant numbers—one hundred dollars, or a zillion dollars, or perhaps a different currency, like gold doubloons—can help avoid getting hung up on specific amounts of money.

Third, all money is not created equal. One million dollars is not simply a million times more valuable than one dollar. Dollars are measured against thresholds. Will your opponent make a profit? Will his financing allow him to pay the new price at all, regardless of whether he wants to? How does this price compare to what his co-workers are getting? Will the new salaries allow your employees to pay their mortgages? Money—and specific dollar amounts—almost always comes attached to specific needs, as well as emotional goals and un-goals. As a result, *a specific dollar value is itself almost never the true top-level goal.*

If you treat every dollar the same as the prior dollar, you will not understand the motivations of your opponent, and you will fail. Do not get distracted by the dollar signs. You have to get past the money to get to the real goals standing behind.

You must comprehend the entire mosaic of motivations, not just your own. Understanding your opponent's goals, un-goals, and cliffs will allow you to identify how their needs relate to yours. Comparing their goals to yours will allow you to identify likely problem spots, potential compromise opportunities, trade-off possibilities, gives, and strategies. Understanding his un-goals and cliffs can provide opportunities to apply selective pressure where it will count the most. Failing to gain this understanding, conversely, dooms you to negotiate in the dark.

# Rule Number 3

## Prepare; Then Prepare Some More

We have all seen the TV shows. Some brilliant lawyer vindicates his wrongfully accused client by cleverly uncovering the key evidence during cross-examination of a hostile witness. He improvises his questions, reacting to what he hears from the witness. It seems he has a quick response and a clever rejoinder for everything.

Reality is not like that. While lawyers are of course brilliant, winning a trial—or a negotiation—is the result of preparation, not improvisation. You will overwhelm your opponent with your understanding of the subject matter, not with your quick wit. High school debate teams understand this, although to an absurd degree—these contests have become little more than high-speed regurgitation of researched data. But as silly as those debates may seem, they demonstrate an important point: The winning team is usually selected based on the strength of their pre-debate research, not their quick wit in the moment. So it is in court and the boardroom as well. To be a successful negotiator, you must prepare. And then prepare some more.

### KNOWING THE KNOWLEDGE

There are two elements to knowledge: the knowledge itself, and the knowledge of the knowledge. Knowing something is useless if you have no confidence in your knowledge. You must not only know the subject matter, but you must know that you know it. You must *know* that you are right.

Be sure. Be very sure.

If you are merely explaining something, or lecturing on a subject, you certainly need a solid understanding of the material, but if you are to negotiate something your very grasp on reality will be under attack. Unless you have complete confidence in your understanding of the relevant facts and circumstances, you will falter as your opponent casts doubt on your knowledge, your competence, and your intelligence.

Let us imagine that you approach a car purchase with lots of research under your belt. You have determined the invoice price for your car of choice. You have determined that $500 over invoice is a reasonable price for the car. You know that this price is all you should pay to the dealer. You will pay tax, title, and license fees, but no undercoating charge, destination charge, stocking fee, or other dealer markup. You have determined this from several independent sources. You are prepared. You are confident.

Or at least you thought you were. After you present your offer to the salesman, he starts talking about the destination charge and the undercoating. You politely inform him that you are not interested in paying for those. Without missing a beat, the salesman explains that the destination charge is "completely standard," and the undercoating is already on the car, so it is only fair that you pay for it.

You object that your information is that neither of those are things that you should be paying for. The salesman simply shrugs and says that you have been misinformed.

And you are stumped. After all, he is a professional, and deals with these things every day. Surely he knows better than some website and your brother-in-law? Maybe these things *are* standard?

His complete confidence in his knowledge, along with your lack of confidence, has rendered your knowledge useless. It no longer matters whether the destination charge is or is not "standard." It does not even matter whether you are right or wrong. What matters is that you do not *know* whether you are right or wrong. Knowledge without confidence is not really knowledge at all, and will do you little good in a negotiation.

You absolutely *must* know your stuff. There is no substitute for preparation. But you need more than mere preparation—you need preparation to the point of confidence.

## READ UP

Preparation requires work. Mostly, it requires reading. Read the contract, the offer, the statute, the associated correspondence, the research. Study your issues lists, your goals, their goals, and the interactions among all of those. Learn it all well. You do not have to memorize everything—but it wouldn't hurt. When your opponent points to the correspondence from May, will you know that the same issue was also addressed in correspondence from June? Depending on the nature of the negotiations, you may not have an opportunity to re-review all the correspondence before responding. Knowledge that is not ready when needed does you little good.

> As a junior associate I was working on a small piece of a large acquisition. At one point I was asked to contact my counterpart on the other side and "discuss" the assignment provision in one of the minor documents.
>
> I was very excited. An opportunity to negotiate! I was determined to trounce my opponent, and I prepared very thoroughly. Before I called opposing counsel, I practically had the entire contract memorized.
>
> I boldly fired off my opening salvo with gusto, confidently expecting prompt surrender—or at least victory following a perfunctory battle. Instead, my opponent simply noted that my position was inconsistent with the assignment provision in the Stock Purchase Agreement, and it was important that the two agreements were consistent.
>
> Ah, yes—the Stock Purchase Agreement. A document I had *not* read in preparation for the negotiation.

Some negotiations are like open-book exams. You will have access to all your materials, with some ability to look things up as you go. In these situations memorization is less useful than deep familiarity with the issues and the ability to quickly locate the specific information required for any given point. Other negotiations are more like closed-book exams, and you will have limited opportunity to consult your files. In these situations you must have all the relevant knowledge in your head or in your hands.

Research the issue. Be up on recent studies, news items, developing trends. You must know the "official" files of the negotiation, but this alone is not enough. Business negotiations do not exist in a closed universe. Don't just rely on the documents at hand. If you can bring in "outside" information and knowledge, this will be a tremendous advantage. Anything you know that your opponent does not is an advantage. Similarly, research is an essential defensive requirement, because your opponent is certain to have researched the matter. When your opponent mentions that UCC 9-305 applies, you will be helpless before him if you do not know what that means. In essence, you have to become your own expert on the matter at hand—either that, or bring somebody who is.

## KNOW WHAT YOU DON'T KNOW

…which leads to an important caveat: The law is a team sport, and that includes negotiations. You need not—and should not—and *cannot*—try to be expert on all things that could come into play in your negotiations. If there are important tax issues, consult a tax lawyer, or bring him with you (assuming you are not a tax lawyer yourself). If a complex tax issue comes up that you cannot properly address yourself, tell your opponent that the issue will have to wait until you can consult with your expert. Yes, this will cost you some credibility, but unless you appear to be punting on every issue the credibility loss will be small. The credibility loss for being wrong about the tax issue, on the other hand, will not be small.

"I don't know" will cost you some credibility (and will cost you more each time you use it), but "I was wrong" will cost you a lot of credibility, and will be fatal if used repeatedly.

This is particularly challenging for beginners, because experience—which each of us lack at first—is important to understand the expectations of other participants. Lack of experience makes it difficult for the beginner to have the proper context during the negotiation. To some extent this handicap cannot be skirted, because the only way to fully overcome lack of experience is…experience, which takes time. There is hope for the beginner, however. Combating inexperience starts with preparation, but it also requires admitting that you are inexperienced. Then be frank with a more experienced colleague, and pick their brain early and often. During negotiation sessions, be cautious about agreeing to anything. Yes, you will suffer for not being able to make snap decisions, but not as much as you will suffer for making the wrong decisions. There is no shortcut past inexperience, but there are quicker (or slower) routes, and you can minimize the damage during the journey.

Preparation by understanding the facts and the law is one thing—preparing for the issues is something else entirely. As part of the goal-identification exercise from Rule #1 ("What Are You Trying To Achieve?") and Rule #2 ("What Are *They* Trying To Achieve?") you also need to identify the arguments you intend to make in

> **Pro Tip:** When preparing, focus as much on facts related to your opponent's goals as those related to your own goals.

support of your goals, as well as likely arguments to be made by your opponents in support of their goals or as attacks on your goals. You need to identify and develop responses to those likely arguments from your opponents, as well as responses to their responses. Play the exchanges out in your mind.

If you are surprised by any fact your opponent brings up, you did not prepare well enough. If you are surprised by any argument your opponent makes, you did not prepare well enough.

Develop your position on each major issue, including opening positions, fall-back positions, and last-ditch position. Failure to identify your positions ahead of time is a certain path to not getting what you want. Have team meetings to discuss issues and positions—even if you are the only one present at the "meeting." Write your positions down, and make sure you understand them—and vet them with your client. You do not want to be inventing compromises on the spot. You do not want to be doing *anything* on the spot.

## PRACTICE MAKES LESS STUPID

Test your arguments. A popular rookie mistake is to plan out all the clever things you are going to say during the negotiation, only to discover that your arguments fail miserably when put into practice. Arguments and clever retorts are, like pick-up lines, among the things that sound better in your head than when said out loud.

This underscores—again—the importance of complete preparation. Research not only the issues and the subject matter, but also your arguments. Most arguments, on almost any issue, have been made before. This stands to be re-emphasized: *You are not special.*

I'm sorry, but you just aren't. You are not a precious snowflake. You are not at the cutting edge of thought in your field. You are not the great innovator. Every thought you have may be new to you, but it is virtually certain that the thought has been had before by somebody else, and equally certain that it has been responded to as well.

Therefore...*prepare.* Do not stockpile your "secret" arguments in your mind, planning to bust them out at the key moment to the stunned surprise and amazement of everyone at the meeting. That is a recipe for disaster (and personal embarrassment). More often than not, your brilliant argument is old hat, and quite frequently it will end up being just plain silly. Negotiation is not about brilliant new arguments, but about familiar elements applied with great preparation and organization.

Instead, research your positions. Review your arguments. If possible, run through the main arguments during pre-negotiation discussions. Pick the brains of more experienced negotiators. Practice your arguments on random passers-by if you have to. See how people respond, and take note of responses and counter-arguments. But *do not go in blind* with surprise arguments. That is not preparation—that is intentional *un*-preparation, and it is a *very* bad idea.

Experienced negotiation professionals take this point seriously. When the stakes are high enough, litigators will even stage entire mock trials as dress rehearsals, just to make sure that all points and arguments are reviewed, evaluated, and vetted. While a "mock negotiation" may not be practical in most instances, the central principle remains: Test your arguments before the actual negotiation. It is quite common for a negotiation team to review arguments and counters before a meeting or call, with participants playing Devil's Advocate to each other to plot out the course of the exchange. You should do so as well whenever possible. You are now playing in the big leagues. You are negotiating with the professionals. You *are* the professional.

Act accordingly.

All those clever rejoinders you see on TV? They are possible, and they can be yours. You too can make improvised, off-the-cuff witty remarks—if you practice them beforehand as part of your thorough preparation for the meeting. Preparation does not mean dull. Preparation means effective.

If your client is surprised by any fact you bring up, then you did not prepare well enough. If your client is surprised by any argument you make, then you did not prepare well enough. If you are surprised by your own facts and arguments, then you most certainly did not prepare well enough.

# Rule Number 4

# It's All About Credibility

Negotiation is a social exercise. And specifically because negotiation is a social exercise, credibility is a prerequisite to success. If you have credibility, people will respect and believe you—including your opponents. If you do not have credibility, everything is an uphill battle. Every statement must be proved, every claim will be challenged. If you have credibility, that credibility is contagious. Your experts will gain credibility from having been introduced by you. Less time will be spent reviewing documents you have drafted. Opponents will begin to adopt a "transparent" negotiation posture, since they believe you are such a credible opponent and will not take advantage of them. If you affirmatively lack credibility, that is also contagious. Your experts will not be trusted, your documents will be scrutinized, your opponents will be cautious and cagey. In the worst case, others will simply refuse to deal with you entirely, and both you and your client will be the losers.

Credibility does not guarantee success, but without credibility you will almost surely fail. Some amount of credibility is absolutely essentially to successful negotiations. With extra credibility you have a tremendous advantage. Any action detrimental to your credibility is a bad idea, and you should seize opportunities to enhance your credibility.

## Be Cool…At Least A Little

There are different kinds of credibility involved in negotiations. The first is your own personal credibility—essentially your social standing in the group. A range of antisocial behaviors will cost you personal credibility. Rudeness and name-calling are of course out, but even lesser social infractions like general grumpiness or failure to join the group for dinner will cost you. Negotiation is a social exercise. You must be social.

If you have lost all personal credibility, or if you are anti-social (or just obnoxious), you will become the enemy. Your opponent will now try to defeat you rather than make the deal or honestly consider your points. Defeating you has now become an un-goal for others, and the negotiations have become combat. While this may distract your opponent from his goals (which is theoretically an advantage for you), it will also obstruct you from your goals (which decidedly is not an advantage for you). The negotiation is not about you. Do not give your opponent a reason to make it about you.

---

Early in my career I was involved in protracted negotiations for a multi-party financing. Each day was spent in a large conference room with 20 + people, and most evenings various subgroups would go to dinner.

During one dinner, two opposing attorneys dominated the table in an extended discussion on the finer points of butchering and dressing meat, thereby stifling an otherwise pleasant evening. Their *faux pas* was emblematic of serial violations of social etiquette, and the rest of us viewed them generally as goofy and out of touch.

Later in the week the negotiations moved to an ERISA issue, which was presented by one of those two. It was the first time this attorney had directly participated in the negotiations. After he had stated his claim and reasoning at length, the lead negotiator on our side simply dismissed it with "No," and then casually moved on to the next item on the agenda.

No one on their side came to his defense. Right or wrong, his position was tainted by his lack of personal credibility.

---

Instead, give your opponent cause to respect you. For the opposite is also true: If you can impress your opponent with your nobility or friendliness, she will be more inclined to want to please you. Spend a few minutes at the beginning of the negotiation session with small talk. Establish rapport with the other side. Work in a friendly word or two during tense moments. Not only do you not want to become the enemy, but you have an opportunity to create a different un-goal for your opponent: the desire to please you. It does not take much to be considered a "nice guy." And we have all been taught from childhood to be nice to nice guys, or at least not to be mean to nice guys. Positive rapport is a powerful tool.

Therefore: *Be* a nice guy. Don't cheat. Be honest and honorable. Pay particular attention to Rule #5 ("Take The High Road"), and *take* the high road, when you can. Play by the rules. How hard is that?

## WHEN IN ROME...

But...the rules vary. Play by the right rules. Understand the social context and informal rules of your situation. Do not get stuck in a static view of what is appropriate and what is not. In a cooperative business negotiation, for instance, clever verbal traps and maneuvers are usually frowned upon, even though those same traps are standard in more-structured contexts. Similarly, a fair amount of "puffery" can be expected in sales negotiations, but only very little puffery is appropriate in business discussions. Each of these transgressions could cost you credibility if used in the wrong context. Each geographic location, each industry, each social context—they all have their own unique and specific rules for what is and is not acceptable behavior. You need to understand these rules—especially those described in Rule #11 ("Understand the Environment")—and apply the correct ones.

> **Pro Tip:** When researching your opponent, look for personal details that can help you establish rapport.

## REMEMBER WHOSE TEAM YOU ARE ON

You need to manage to be the good guy while still zealously pursuing the goals of your client. Don't let the pursuit of your personal credibility become an un-goal. Don't confuse the credibility boost from being a nice guy with the un-goal of pleasing others.

---

I was negotiating an agreement between two large energy-trading companies. Everyone at the table (other than I) was a sophisticated and experienced energy trader.

The pricing structure for the agreement was a complex mathematical formula. At one stage my client suggested some revisions to the pricing formula that would clearly favor our side, but the benefits were insidiously hidden in the math.

My client was confident that the other side was not clever enough to catch the effect of the change, and wanted to introduce it as a minor cleanup.

I was concerned that this sneakiness would lead to significant credibility loss if discovered, and told the client as much. The client laughed and assured me that attempting to outsmart each other in this fashion was not only within the "rules" of the industry, but practically expected. Trying to discover the other side's tricks was part of the "thrill of the hunt." It was almost a game to them, with the players trying to outsmart each other.

The client told me that he could guarantee that the other side was always trying to slip one by on us as well, and was easily able to point to instances in other transactions where they had made apparently innocent changes that in fact were anything but.

Context matters.

---

You must also distinguish between "internal" credibility (your credibility as to your clients and colleagues) and "external" credibility (your credibility as to your opponents). It is possible to improve or damage one without affecting the other. Playing dumb, for instance, can be a powerful tactic—but at some expense to your personal credibility. If your client knows what you are doing, however, then it is only your external credibility that is damaged. Your internal credibility remains unharmed, or even improved.

## APPEAR REASONABLE

Beyond personal credibility, you need to protect your issue credibility, or your appearance of reasonableness. You need to convey to your opponent that your positions are rational and reasonable. Your opponent needs to know that if he could but come up with the perfect argument, or the perfect price, you would surrender your position. Even positions that you have declared sacrosanct must be theoreti-

> **Pro Tip:** Playing dumb is not only a good way to gain information, but also an effective tool when applying Rule #17 ("Nail Down The Weasel").

cally moveable. If you do the functional equivalent of sticking your fingers in your ears and shouting "LALALALALALALA…" while your opponent is talking, he will stop talking—or at least stop talking *to you*—and you will accomplish nothing. It matters not how much of a nice guy you are. If your positions appear unreasonable, then your negotiation will fail.

This does not mean that you have to be willing to abandon your positions at the drop of a hat. It means that you must be willing to abandon your positions if the circumstances are right, or willing to reconsider your positions in light of new facts or positions – or at least *appear* to be willing to do so. Virtually any position can be changed given the right circumstances. You need to be open to that idea, and make sure that your opponents know this. You can declare certain positions unassailable and certain of your opponents' propositions as "non-starters," but those declarations must be based in reason. And for "non-starters" to be based in reason, there must be some theoretical circumstance where they *are* subject to change. Blindly, irrationally, and stubbornly sticking to points for the sole purpose of sticking to points will cause your opponents to label you blind, irrational, and stubborn, and they will not bother to talk to you at all. Fail.

The truth, of course, is that most issues are not truly "non-starters." Most things we declare as "must-haves" are in truth only "really-wants." Almost everything has a price. When we say "non-starter," we really mean "not acceptable without significant restructuring of the transaction." A little hyperbole about the importance of a point is not necessarily a bad thing, but we must not literally believe our own puffery.

For the same reason, you must be willing to admit to a mistake. Few things will reduce your credibility faster than clinging to a point that has been conclusively shown to be incorrect. This is a major social cliff. If you were wrong or misinformed, or made a mistake—admit it. Everyone is wrong sometimes. So long as you don't make a habit of it, the credibility loss will usually be manageable. They will think a *lot* less of you if you fail to fess up, however. And in certain circumstances, nobly admitting to your error can *improve* your personal credibility as well as issue credibility. Do not squander this opportunity by trying to shelter a frail ego. Protecting your ego is an un-goal. Protecting and increasing your credibility are important intermediate goals and should be pursued, even at some cost to your ego.

> **Pro Tip:** The primary damage from making a mistake is often the damage to your own confidence. Don't let it show.

There is a delicate balance here. You absolutely must maintain a minimum level of credibility, or all is lost. At the same time you must avoid being seduced by your own credibility, and instead keep your eye on the ball. In between those two boundaries is the field where you can seek and play with credibility, but never forget that credibility is a tool and not the goal.

# Rule Number 5

# Take The High Road

This Rule is effectively a continuation of Rule #4 ("It's All About Credibility"), and a special case of that Rule. I am dedicating *two* Rules to credibility management—so far. Take the hint. Credibility is important.

There are a variety of theories about honor in negotiations. Some believe that you should be a saint and set the highest standards of ethical behavior. Others believe that you can and should fight tooth and nail to win, even "cheating" when necessary. Sneaky tricks, traps, and ploys—all just part of the game. Some believe in secrets; others believe in "transparency."

My view is that each of these perspectives is simplistic. Before we can develop a view of what behaviors are and are not permitted or appropriate in any given negotiation, we must return to Rule #1 ("What Are You Trying To Achieve?").

Well, what *are* you trying to achieve?

You are presumably trying to "win" the current exchange and achieve your goals for the negotiation. But…are there likely to be future exchanges, either with this opponent or with her colleagues or acquaintances? Or perhaps this exchange is part of an ongoing relationship? Do you work in a niche practice or industry? Is it important for you to maintain a certain reputation—a certain level of credibility? Credibility loss, even future credibility loss, is a cliff.

Some negotiations truly are isolated instances. A new car purchase could be that way. You could go your entire life without visiting the same dealership twice, let alone dealing with the same salesman twice. But in your professional life this is less likely to be true. You will face the same opponents on multiple occasions. Or you'll face opponents who know of you (or who ask about you). Of equal importance, you will be working with people on *your* side on multiple occasions. Most business negotiations also tend to be ongoing, drawn-out affairs, with plenty of time to build up and capitalize on a reputation within the very same exchange.

> As a junior associate I was managing a large document distribution for a complex acquisition. Different selections of documents were going to different parties, and I mistakenly included an internal draft of a document in the package to opposing counsel.
>
> I discovered this only when opposing counsel called me to ask if I wanted the draft back or if he should have it shredded.
>
> To this day I still think of him as an upstanding and trustworthy man.

What this means for you is that you must have a personal goal to maintain your individual professional credibility, with a longer time horizon than merely the current transaction. Rule #1 ("What Are You Trying to Achieve?") does not require that you sacrifice your professional future to help your clients achieve their immediate goals. While it is true that this is not about you, and your personal goals are usually un-goals in a negotiation for a client, that does not mean that you can have no regard for your own professional credibility. You must be able to live to fight another day.

Moreover, we are attorneys. Some people might expect a certain level of underhandedness from, say, used-car salesmen, but—lawyer jokes notwithstanding—attorneys are held to a higher standard. You will be judged against how others think *an attorney* ought to act, not how they think random business managers ought to act. And, of course, as attorneys we are subject to detailed legal rules of ethics.

As a result, it will usually benefit you to take the high road. Don't cheat. Don't play dirty tricks. Don't do anything that falls outside the boundaries of "good behavior." Almost invariably, these things end up hurting you more than they help. Rule #4 ("It's All About Credibility") is paramount in this context. You must maintain your credibility—but not just to help your clients achieve their goals. You must also preserve your own future status as a credible negotiator.

Beyond the small talk and congenial behavior described in Rule #4, we as attorneys have ample opportunity to rise to a higher level—or fail to rise—and I unabashedly advocate taking the high road when given a choice. This is not about social interactions, but about ethical behavior—motivated entirely by selfish motives, if that's what it takes to get you to behave.

Try to be a beacon of moral righteousness. You will find that this is not only easy, but pays dividends in excess of the effort involved. You can do better than merely avoiding career suicide—you can generate a source of strength. Cynics would have you

> **Pro Tip:** Take confidentiality seriously. Very seriously. Few things unravel client relationships faster than a breach of confidentiality, even if well-intended and "harmless."

believe that taking shortcuts is easy and doing the right thing is difficult (as well as downright foolish). This might be true in some areas, but in a negotiation context the opposite is usually true.

## TAKE THE ROAD MORE TRAVELED

Consider the following example—a classic from many legal ethics discussions:

> You are on a plane, traveling to a negotiation meeting for a large, complicated deal. An hour into the flight you realize that you are sitting directly behind a group from the other side to the negotiation, and they are discussing strategy. (Shame on them.) They are going through their issues lists and strategies, in great detail. This is potentially negotiation gold for you. So what do you do? Do you break out the notepad and recorder? Do you put on your headphones and tune them out? Do you tap them on the shoulder and politely tell them to shut up?

Well, what are you trying to achieve?

Never forget Rule #1. Gaining information is always a goal, so taking action to gain information would seem appropriate. But this intermediate goal is subservient to the higher-level goal of succeeding in the negotiation, and also subservient to your personal goal of having a successful career. By the way, variations on this hypothetical—and the response options— occur constantly in a legal context. Misplaced memos, misguided correspondence, elevator chatter, thin walls—the list goes on. Given how much sensitive information we have, attorneys can sometimes be astonishingly bad at protecting it, and our clients even more so.

Let us see how some of our options in this hypothetical situation work in relation to those goals.

**Option 1: Unrepentantly take careful notes.** This is certainly the most exciting option. You get to take advantage of a big mistake by your opponents, you will have an informational edge during the session, and you get to feel a little 007 about the whole affair. All good things. This, of course, assumes that you won't get caught. Which you will. You almost certainly will get caught.

How can I say that with such confidence? Well, in this particular hypothetical it is almost inevitable that your opponents will spot you at one point or other. Between bathroom stops, disembarking, luggage collecting, and taxi-getting, there are simply too many opportunities for them to catch a glimpse.

The specifics, of course, will vary—but my point is that the chances are you will get caught, regardless of the specific circumstances. Despite your daydreaming, you are not James Bond. This is not a well-planned industrial espionage operation. You have no backup plan, escape route, or inside accomplice. It is just you stumbling upon a lucky opportunity, and just like when you nose through your friend's medicine cabinet, chances are just pretty darn good that you'll be spotted at the worst possible time.

And even if something does not go wrong, even if they some-how never look back and never go to the bathroom on the airplane, and against all odds you make it to the meeting with your secret stash undiscovered, chances are *still* good that you will get caught. Because in the end you have to use this information. And when you start magically predicting their every move, knowing their every limit and fallback position, they are going to figure out that something is up. The better your information, the more spectacular the negotiation results, the better the chance that your opponents will cry foul. The only way that this won't trip you up is if the secret information wasn't that useful anyway, or perhaps wasn't all that secret.

Which leads to another point: preparation. How many secrets can your opponents really have? Much of the information possessed by either party is semi-public anyway. If you paid attention to Rule #3 ("Prepare; Then Prepare Some More"), and you have done your preparation thoroughly, most secret conversations you can overhear will not be all that exciting, or even interesting. While there might be more information to be gleaned, chances are quite good that the content of any covertly gained communication will be mostly stuff you already know, or at least should have known or been able to anticipate with good preparation.

> **Pro Tip:** People expect lawyers to not give away confidential information. When we say "I cannot answer that question," people tend to believe us, and will not necessarily infer that we are hiding something. This works also for questions you simply do not want to answer.

Will there be nuggets of gold in there? Sure, probably…but at what cost? You will have exposed your reputation to potentially great damage for a small amount of information that you may or may not be able to use without alerting everyone to your shenanigans.

But wait—there's more. So far I have discussed only the risk of getting discovered by the other side. If this secret information is any good, it will probably have to be shared with the other members of your own team. They will probably not agree to a shift in strategy based on your "hunch" of unknown origins, so you have to tell them about your clandestine adventures. Will they approve? Will they *all* approve? Your colleagues *and* your clients? Including the senior partners at your firm? Are you sure? Are you sure enough to bet your professional reputation on it?

And even if the client does feel the same way you do and congratulates you on your "aggressive" approach to negotiation, who else will they tell about their secret information and how it was acquired? Will they brag to the other side at the end of the negotiation? Will they tell their co-workers, who might not approve so readily? Once the tale of your doings is out, it is out, and you no longer have any control over this story detailing your lack of professionalism.

**Option 2: Don't listen.** This option seems noble. You do not commit any ethically questionable acts, you get to be a stand-up guy for refusing to take "unfair" advantage of the situation, and you generally get to feel all warm and fuzzy about it.

This option, however, is the dumbest of all.

It is dumb because it carries nearly all of the downsides of Option 1 and Option 3 combined, and you get the benefits of neither (other than that warm and fuzzy feeling). Do you think that your opponents will know that you were not listening when they see you at the baggage pickup? Do you think they will not harbor the same negative feelings toward you as if you actually had been listening? Think again. You might as well have taken notes, since you will pay the price anyway. This, of course, is why I believe that Option 3 is the best choice.

**Option 3: Tap their shoulder.** This last option is simple enough. Tap their shoulder, let them know that you can hear what they are saying, and politely suggest that they hold off on their confidential conversation until they are in a confidential place. Delicately ignore the embarrassed looks, and sit down for the rest of the flight.

As with Option 2, you get the warm and fuzzy feeling of ethical superiority at the cost of secret knowledge, but this time you also get something far more valuable: credit for your ethical superiority.

If a tree behaves ethically in the forest, does anyone care? This is not a book about legal ethics, but a book about effective negotiations. And for ethical behavior to have an impact on your negotiations, people need to know about it. Warm and fuzzy feelings will not help you achieve your goals. Your increased credibility *will.*

## *USE* THE HIGH ROAD

Simply behaving ethically means that you are not behaving *uneth-ically.* This is valuable, since you thereby avoid the risk of being caught behaving unethically. But, as noted, the practical value of ethical behavior in negotiations comes from the credibility you gain from others *knowing* about your ethical behavior. This opens opportunities for you.

Taking the high road can be a matter of career self-defense, but it is also a tool at your disposal for offensive purposes. Perhaps the best part of taking the high road: you can bootstrap credibility. By this I mean that Option 3 works almost as well even if your opponents are discussing the weather rather than their secret strategy. Alerting them to your presence makes you look good even if there are no secrets to glean. This is just free credibility for you. You are accidentally copied on an internal email from opposing counsel? Tell him right away—you get bonus credibility points even if the email was completely harmless. It doesn't matter; you gain anyway.

You don't have to wait to ignore actual trade secrets…you can start ignoring right away. Don't just enter the conference room—knock and announce yourself, so people can stop their confidential conversations. Offer to leave the room when the other side is having a sidebar. You happen to understand the foreign language they are speaking amongst themselves? Let them know before they have a chance to discuss anything important.

There will be countless opportunities for you to be "pre-ethical" like this. Seize them. Make a point of telling people of ethical considerations, even if they perhaps are not really all that important. Do not passively wait for the high road to appear—

*create* the high road if you have to, use it to your advantage, and start racking up those credibility points.

# Rule Number 6

## Sit Down And Shut Up

Most people like to talk. Lawyers *love* to talk. Often, that is one of the main reasons they are lawyers.

This is a good thing—for you.

Whenever *you* are talking, you are giving information away. Whenever you are listening, you are gaining information. By now it should be obvious that information is power. So why are you in such a hurry to give it away?

Several principles come from this simple observation.

### Talk

First, some amount of talking is necessary. Without it you will not be able to convey your requirements and arguments. It is important that you communicate effectively with your opponent. Goals and cliffs must be conveyed effectively (some of them, anyway), and supporting rationale must be argued. Failing to speak, or to speak at the right time, or in the correct fashion, is a fatal error.

But don't overdo it! Anything said more than the minimum required is not likely to work in your favor. This does not mean that you should talk very little—it just means that you should talk no more than necessary. Sometimes a lot of talking is necessary. But do not talk for the sake of talking. Every word that escapes your mouth is another nugget of information given away, and,

> **Pro Tip:** When somebody on the other side is sympathetic to your position, recruit them. Find ways to bring them into the discussion. Elicit their opinions. Make them unwitting allies, and let them argue your point for you.

just as important, every second spent talking is a second spent not listening. Don't be stingy with your words, but don't waste them either. Manage your information. Distribute the information you want to distribute, and not an iota more. The joy of listening to your own voice is an un-goal. Avoid it.

## Don't Talk

Second, do not fill the silence. A long-standing social convention has declared silences bad and dead air an embarrassment. This is a trap and an opportunity, for a negotiation is not a social conversation. When you are finished talking, *stop talking.* If your opponent says nothing, then shut your mouth and bite your tongue. If your opponent is finished talking and you have nothing to say, then don't say anything. There is no prize for filling the awkward silence. To the contrary, the black hole of silence will suck in the undisciplined and force them to say things they should not. The desire to fill the silence can be immense.

Don't do it.

Let your opponent fill that void instead. Simply looking at your opponent with a pensive look on your face (looking bored or inattentive is generally a bad idea in any meeting) is a more powerful argument than whatever vapid thing you were going to say to fill the silence, and is quite likely to prompt verbal diarrhea from your opponent. This does not mean that you should let the proceedings degenerate into a game of "silence," kindergarten-style. It just means that you should remember your goals, and not be distracted by the un-goal of avoiding dead air in conversation. Instead, steer your opponent toward that distraction and smooth her passage.

## Shut Up

Third, do not undermine your own arguments by overstating them, or by restating them, or by re-restating them. When the point is made, stop. Good arguments require a moment to settle.

Don't argue a point already made. If you keep talking after you made your point, your opponent will be listening to whatever filler you are spouting instead of pondering the brilliant insight you meant for her to focus on. And when you finally do stop talking, she will remember the last thing you said, not the better thing you said earlier. Let her have a moment to think about your point. Be quiet—stop distracting her.

> At the beginning of a negotiation session, opposing counsel was explaining their basic position on the major issues. I was listening carefully and not saying anything.
>
> After he finished I sat quietly, taking notes and contemplating the information we had just received. I was not intentionally being quiet. I just had a fairly large amount of information to digest.
>
> Opposing counsel did not appear to enjoy the silence. After a few moments he started expanding on what he had told us. It quickly became apparent that he was now off-script, as he started filling in the details of internal discussions and disagreements and other nifty tidbits that he almost certainly had not intended to share.
>
> At this point my silence became very intentional, and I just looked at him as he continued to talk. Thankfully, my client also recognized the moment and said nothing. Opposing counsel kept talking.
>
> At one point he stopped himself, looked at me and said, "You haven't said anything. I should probably stop talking, shouldn't I?"
>
> I did not respond.
>
> Having thus recognized that he was making a mistake, opposing counsel nevertheless went right back to telling us *even more* about their internal discussions.

## LISTEN

Last but not least, listen. Really *listen*. Creating an opportunity for your opponent to talk too much does you no good if you don't pay attention when he does. Closing your mouth is not sufficient; you must also open your ears. Most of the nuggets you will hear during filled silences will be unintentional, and will pass you by if you are not paying attention.

Listening isn't just for dead air, either. Pay attention when your opponents are speaking amongst themselves. Endless insights will be gained by these quasi-sidebars. Listen to the arguments each is making. Watch the body language. See who is tilting in your direction, and who is resisting. Identify who is the real boss, and who the boss looks to for advice. Don't interrupt (usually), but let the drama play out for your benefit.

The same goes when people are talking to you. When the other side is telling you their goals, pay attention! This is important stuff. Their goals—and their cliffs—are just as important as your goals and cliffs. Everything your opponent says is important, and you must pay attention.

Do not spend your listening time mentally preparing your response. Do not spend your listening time congratulating yourself on your brilliant argument, or getting distracted by the excellent rejoinder you are planning. Do not spend your listening time organizing lunch.

> **Pro Tip:** When a member of the other team is actually arguing your point for you, let them. Don't help.

Spend your listening time *listening*. Listening gains you information. Listening is at least as important as talking, and you will surely fail as a negotiator if you do not listen well.

# Rule Number 7

# Master The Art of Appeasement

Appeasement, as a negotiation strategy, has gotten a bit of a bad rap. Detractors claim that it does not work, and point to how poorly this strategy worked when Chamberlain tried it with Hitler.

Appeasement has come to be synonymous with weakness, with poor decision-making ability. This is unfortunate, for nothing could be further from the truth. Appeasement is a powerful technique when used properly, and should be in the toolkit of every negotiator.

Appeasement is the art of using an opponent's cliffs against him. You threaten the cliff and bribe with small goals, all the while keeping the large goals for yourself. It is seductively effective and difficult to defend against.

## POWER

Typically in a negotiation relationship one party has more immediate power than the other. An employer has more immediate power than an employee—the employer can change working conditions, pay, or benefits; can promote, demote, discipline; and so forth. A bank has more immediate power than a loan applicant—the applicant needs the money, while the bank already has the money. A car dealer has more immediate power than a purchaser—the dealer has better information, more experience, and can spread risk across numerous transactions. The government has more immediate power than the population—the government can change laws, taxes, etc. The police negotiator has more immediate power than the hostage-takers; the U.S. has more immediate power than North Korea.

At the same time, the other party, the "weaker" party, typically holds a large weapon, but an unpleasant one: a "nuclear option" (usually a metaphor). The employee can quit (or join with other employees to strike), the car purchaser or loan applicant can leave, the population can revolt, the hostage-taker can kill the hostages, North Korea might actually nuke something.

This nuclear option is typically something costly to the weaker party as well as to the stronger party. It is a cliff, for both parties. The weaker party does not really want to commit to it, but will if forced to. The main negotiation strategy of the weaker party is often to threaten (implicitly or explicitly) to exercise the nuclear option.

## SING A SOOTHING LULLABY

Throughout history, a strategy of revolutionaries has been what might be called "crisis maximization." This strategy consists of making things as *bad* as possible for the population, so as to essentially force them into open revolt. By intentionally disrupting the government's attempts at compromise, the revolutionaries make the nuclear option (*i.e.,* revolution) seem less unattractive in comparison. This strategy has also been used by labor leaders to push union members towards a strike, for instance. It is essentially brinksmanship, but aimed at your own side instead of at your opponents, to unite your people and spur them to action.

Appeasement is the reverse of crisis maximization. It is crisis *minimization,* aimed at the other side. It is the art of throwing crumbs at your opponents to stop them from exercising their nuclear option. It is the calm soothing of tensions, the dousing of fires—barely.

In a government context, the government lowers taxes just enough to avoid revolution. The demands of the population are not quite met, but enough crumbs are tossed around that revolution is not quite justified; it is too unattractive in light of the tasty if tiny new crumbs.

In the employment context, the employer does not actually grant the requested salary hike, but increases salaries just enough that quitting or striking just does not quite seem worth it. Or the employer installs a new game machine, or paints the lunchroom, or extends medical leave benefits, or grants some other lesser goodie. Crumbs. Appeasement.

In the car dealer context, the dealer will not agree to your price, but will instead throw in the undercoating at no charge, or maybe the premium sound system at cost—just enough that you do not want to walk away from the deal and have to start all over again. Crumbs. Appeasement.

> My client had hired a contractor to build an industrial facility.
>
> The construction contract was brutally one-sided in our favor, which the contractor was slowly realizing during construction. Halfway through the project, the contractor determined that they were unlikely to make a profit on the project, and could face a significant loss.
>
> The contractor approached my client demanding changes to the contract, threatening to walk off the job. My client faced economic disaster if there was a substantial construction delay. We needed the contractor to stay on the job.
>
> We responded to the contractor's demand with a small amendment to the contract, limiting the contractor's downside (based on our calculations, this limit was unlikely to come into play, and therefore relatively harmless to us). At the same time we expressed our confidence that we would be successful in court if needed.
>
> The cost of litigation was thus greater than the worst-case scenario under the contract, and the contractor grudgingly proceeded to finish the project at little or no profit.

If the weaker party exercises the nuclear option, it will suffer significant negative consequences itself. The nuclear option could kill the deal, lead to loss of employment, or, in the case of our crisis-maximizing revolutionaries, war. Whatever it is, it is a cliff—something that the weaker party would rather avoid—and as such it is an exploitable weakness by the stronger party.

But for appeasement to work, certain conditions must apply: The "strong" party must have crumbs to give. The other party must be "weaker" in terms of immediate power, and have relatively few options for compromise, while possessing some type of unpleasant nuclear option—unpleasant to both parties. The nuclear option must be a significant cliff for both parties. If the weaker party is not afraid to use the nuclear option, then it is not the weaker party. If the stronger party does not fear the nuclear option, then the stronger party holds all the cards and need not waste time appeasing. It is important to understand these conditions. Attempting appeasement without the presence of *all* of these conditions will not work, and can have significant negative consequences.

This combination of circumstances sounds rare, but in fact is quite common in a negotiation. Abandoning the deal is almost always an option, and is usually unpleasant enough for both parties to make it "nuclear." At the same time, almost by definition one party has more power than the other; it does not take much of a power differential to support some degree of appeasement.

The first trick is figuring out whether you are the strong or the weak party, and just how strong and weak each party is. This is not always obvious, and can change in the middle of negotiations. It is also subject to emotion, psychology, and social pressures, un- goals, and cliffs: If the stronger party acts weak, it *is* weak. If the weaker party acts strong—and that apparent strength is accepted at face value—then for the purposes of that negotiation at least, it *is* strong.

If the other party is the strong party, then you are not appeasing…you're getting bullied. Appeasement only works from a position of relative strength. If you do not have that strength, do not attempt appeasement. But if you *are* in this position of strength, where your principal concern is your opponent's nuclear option, you need to use your strength, and one of the ways to leverage your strength is by appeasement.

After you have identified the strong and weak parties, understand the nuclear option. That means identify it (don't just assume a nuclear option, or a lack of one), but it also means understand just how scary it is to each party. It is easy to project your own fear onto your opponent, and assume that the nuclear option frightens her as much as it does you. It is easy—it is also a mistake.

Remember Rule #2 ("What Are *They* Trying to Achieve"). Your opponent is not simply your mirror image. Understand how your opponent feels about the nuclear option, not just how you would feel if you were her—because you are not her, and she isn't you.

## LESSONS OF HISTORY

Whenever the word "appeasement" is used, the words "Hitler" and "Chamberlain" are usually not far behind. The dangers of failing to fully understand the necessary conditions to appeasement can be seen in that most famous historical example.

Here is the mostly-conventional view of the appeasement of 1938: Chamberlain let Hitler have Sudetenland (and Austria) without making too much fuss, figuring that this would satisfy Hitler's bloodlust and thus avoid war.

This didn't work, of course, and here is why: Hitler was not afraid of war. In fact, large-scale war was his plan all along. Sudetenland was an appetizer, not appeasement. Chamberlain's first mistake was in believing that Hitler shared his fear of war, and that Hitler also wanted to avoid war. Chamberlain attempted to bribe Hitler with Sudetenland while subtly threatening war if Hitler kept pressing the issue. Because the weaker party was not afraid of the nuclear option, appeasement was inappropriate and ineffective.

But that isn't all. Together France and England were militarily stronger than Germany, even at the end of the 1930s. Yet they didn't *believe* they were. They certainly did not *act* as if they were. In the context of negotiation, that means they were not the strong party, which made them the weak party. Chamberlain, for example, had to go to Hitler. Weak. Chamberlain wanted peace at all costs. Weak. So even though England and France were objectively stronger, that strength was irrelevant. In their negotiation, perception became reality. This is a key point in negotiation. Objective reality is just one part of the total reality that applies in negotiation. Appeasement only works from a position of strength—real *and* perceived. If you are the stronger party, you have to act the part. If you do not act like a strong party, then you are not a strong party. If you attempt appeasement without real *and* perceived strength, your appeasement effort will fail and you will only encourage your opponent instead.

So much for the conventional historical account. In the context of this Rule, 1938 was actually a lesson in how effective appeasement can be—and because it was done so forcefully yet subtly, decades later we still haven't caught on: it was Hitler who appeased Chamberlain.

While Hitler *should have been* the weaker party, he was in fact the stronger party...because his counterparts let him be. Chamberlain's weakness made Hitler the stronger party, and Chamberlain's fear of war made for a good nuclear option—and thus an easy means of appeasement. It was *Chamberlain* who was appeased: he got a meaningless signature, while Hitler kept what he intended all along. Hitler wanted to avoid premature allied military action, sure, yet the nuclear option was far more frightening to England and France—to the point where Chamberlain was appeasable with a mere signature.

> **Pro Tip:** Not sure who the "weak" party is? Strong parties don't ask for concessions.

I therefore view that there were *two* appeasement attempts in 1938. One succeeded brilliantly; one failed spectacularly. Both provide valuable lessons.

Here's how we might list the conventional wisdom:

    Strong party: Chamberlain
    Weak party: Hitler
    Appeasement crumb: Sudetenland
    Nuclear option: All-out war

And here is the lesser-known appeasement:

    Strong party: Hitler
    Weak party: Chamberlain
    Appeasement crumb: Signature
    Nuclear option: Deterrent use of military force

Both of these appeasement events are instructive, because they show the insidious effectiveness of which appeasement is capable *and* the price of failure when the would-be appeaser does not fully think the appeasement through. Appeasement is powerful, but also dangerous. Deploy with care.

## Divide and Conquer

Appeasement works by sowing doubt and dissent. Exercising the nuclear option requires resolute determination. All you need to do is undermine that determination. When your opponent is a single individual, you need to place doubt in her mind. Give her some crumbs, while subtly reminding her how unpleasant the nuclear option really is. If your opponent is a group, or multiple representatives of an entity, appeasement works even better. In this case you can sow dissent in their ranks. If some degree of consensus is required to exercise the nuclear option, then appeasement is powerful indeed, and you will need to throw even-smaller crumbs to create the minimum required level of doubt in the collective minds of your opponents.

> **Pro Tip:** When appeasing, never give the impression that crumbs are cheap for you. Never admit how much their nuclear option frightens you.

This is an essential point. Overwhelmingly, in business negotiations big decisions are made by committee, and this is particularly true of nuclear options. It will be rare that any single individual at the negotiation table has the unilateral authority to walk away from the deal. There will be great pressure from within (or above) to arrive at *some* agreement. When deal momentum of Rule #19 ("Watch The Tide") has set in, this pressure can be overwhelming. You must leverage this pressure to your advantage.

## WHEN PLAYING WITH FIRE...

Appeasement is also seductive to the user, however: It tempts you to use it inappropriately—not just by failing to understand the necessary conditions, but also by luring you into underestimating the cost of your crumbs. When this happens, you end up appeasing yourself instead of your opponent. You must be vigilant. Appeasement leads to peace and quiet, and we all love peace and quiet. "Peace and quiet" is an un-goal. The purpose of appeasement, remember, is not to grant all the requests from the other side; it is merely to give just enough to keep them pacified. Barely. You just want to keep the customer from walking out on the deal; you do not want to close the deal on his terms.

It is important to gauge the price of appeasement. Appeasement requires you to give small things away, and care should be taken that you give as little as possible, and that what you give is an acceptable loss. Only when pacification can be purchased for a reasonable price in crumbs is appeasement a wise strategy. If your opponent is headed for the nuclear option anyway, then don't waste your time or crumbs on appeasement efforts. If your opponent is too weak or committed to exercise the nuclear option, then give little—perhaps skipping appeasement altogether in favor of outright strong-arming. Appeasement is not about charity, but about buying compliance at the best possible price.

It is therefore essential to remember to stop giving. It can be incredibly tempting to continue granting your opponent's requests—it seems to make him so happy! But that takes us back to the un-goal of pleasing everyone, and this un-goal is particularly tempting when appeasing, since you are already in a giving mode and feeling generous. If you lose discipline you will quickly have appeased yourself into giving too much away, which is the source of another criticism frequently levied at appeasement—that all it accomplishes is giving things away for no apparent gain. If you are not careful, this is exactly what will happen.

Appeasement is the art of saying yes to small, unimportant requests (or better yet, proactively throwing crumbs of your choosing), while standing firm on "No" to the big requests and keeping your opponent from jumping off that cliff and exercising his nuclear option. You have to trade small gives for big takes, and if you keep making small gives indefinitely, there will eventually be nothing left of value for you to give—or keep.

# Rule Number 8

## ...And Also The Salami

Appeasement is fundamentally a defensive tactic. Its purpose is to maintain your position of strength, to preserve the status quo, keep what you have, and stop your opponent from going off the cliff. It is in essence stalling, and works wonders if you like the way things are.

If you want to improve your position, however, then the Salami is for you. Simply put, doing the Salami is getting the whole salami—or at least most of it—one thin slice at a time. You want a $5/hour raise for your union members? Don't ask for a $5 raise. Instead, ask for a $0.50 raise with every new contract. Also make sure to charge for any concessions you make. The employer wants to add job duties for some employees? Sure, no problem—if there is a $1 raise for all employees. The employer doesn't want to renovate the cafeteria? No problem, if everybody gets an additional $0.50 raise. Each individual request seems relatively minor, harmless, and reasonable, but collectively they add up.

The Salami is the offensive counterpart to appeasement. It is also a wonderful defense against appeasement. If you think you are being appeased by your opponent, stick it to him with the Salami. Your opponent throws you a crumb, ask for two more crumbs. If he doesn't offer a crumb for a while, go ahead and ask for some crumbs anyway. Pretty soon you will have the whole loaf (or salami, as the case may be), and your opponent won't even know he's being taken. It's just one small slice, right? Not a big deal, really. Just one more. One. Small. Slice.

Salami-ing works because each request is so small that refusing would seem unreasonable. It makes your opponent look bad to kill the deal over a tiny little itty bitty issue like this one. Only a spiteful, unreasonable person would refuse such a modest request.

This can put you in a difficult position when facing the Salami. Defending against the Salami requires one of two approaches:

either re-characterize the Salami request as a big important concession (instead of a thin slice), or simply stare down your opponent
and call him on the Salami-ing that you know is going on. The former approach requires a scenario where you can recast the
requested concession as important without looking irrational. The
latter approach requires you to be a position of great strength, and
also requires significant credibility, because you are essentially
declaring your willingness to kill the deal over a "small" issue.

> A client had just completed an acquisition of a manufactur-
> ing facility. The acquired facility was a union shop, and the
> client had no prior experience with unions.
>
> Intending to get off to a good start with his new union
> employees, the client asked the union representative to give
> him a list of all the union's requests—wages, schedules, sick-
> days, on-site conveniences, etc.—and the representative did
> so. Nothing on the list seemed particularly unreasonable to
> the client who, after reviewing the list, agreed to implement
> every single item. The client assumed this would be the end
> of it.
>
> A week later, the union representative presented him
> with a new list of demands.

If your opponent is trying to appease you, and is therefore in a
giving mood, take advantage of that. Keep the implicit threat of the
nuclear option alive, and raise the price of keeping it off the table.
Remember that your opponent does not like the nuclear option
either, and if she thinks you can be bribed, then let her bribe you—
but at a higher cost than she intended.

Salami-ing is not random. Always remember to ask yourself
what you are trying to achieve. You are not just collecting
crumbs—you are working toward a specific goal: The whole salami, or as much of it as you can get. To successfully deploy the
Salami you absolutely must retain a solid grip on Rule #1 ("What
Are You Trying To Achieve?"). Get the concessions you want and
need, not just whatever concessions are offered. Take hold of your

opponent's giving energy and redirect it. If the dealer offers you free undercoating, see if maybe you can't have free maintenance instead. If the employer offers to fix up the lunchroom, trade that for a $2 raise.

As with appeasement, take care not to fall into your own trap. It is easy to get excited because you got two crumbs instead of just the one that was offered, but a bad deal is still a bad deal. Stay

> **Pro Tip:** The Salami cannot be obvious. Every request for a slice should appear independently justified.

on course, and remember what you are trying to achieve. You measure success not relative to your opponent's initial offer, and not by how many crumbs you collect, but by whether you are achieving your *goals.*

You might think you were quite clever to get free maintenance, but if you still paid too much for the car, you didn't Salami your opponent—you just got appeased.

# RULE NUMBER 9

# BRING CREDIBILITY TO THE TABLE

Credibility is not only something you need and want, but can also be a weapon or a shield for your intentional use. You worked hard to earn that credibility—now *use* it. And don't just use it to support your own positions. The credibility of your opponent is also important, and using your credibility to attack his can be a valuable tactic, if done carefully and within the bounds of the social context.

Credibility arguments essentially stack your credibility up against that of your opponent. There are countless varieties of credibility arguments. I will describe a few, but there are many more, and you should strive to identify them when you see them in action. The central theme will be that these arguments succeed or fail in significant part on the strength of the relative credibility of the opponents. If you face an argument that appears to have relatively little basis in fact or logic, you are probably looking at a credibility argument.

Because the effectiveness of credibility arguments depends on your credibility, you should consider the landscape before barging in. If you believe your credibility is not as good as your opponent's, then you want to avoid these types of arguments, and instead build up your credibility with cold, hard facts. On the other hand, if you believe you have a credibility advantage, you can use that advan-

> **Pro Tip:** Not sure who has the most credibility? Then it probably isn't you.

tage to force resolution of issues in your favor, even where the underlying substance of the issue may not have been so favorable to you.

When facing credibility arguments, defending against them usually involves one of two approaches: Facing them head-on by pitting your own credibility against your opponent's credibility, or doing an end-run on credibility with facts and logic. The latter approach can be difficult at times, because credibility arguments are best deployed precisely when there are precious few facts and logic to be had, but should always be explored as an option. The former approach requires credibility, and lots of it.

Of course, when playing credibility games it is important to observe the rules of credibility. Inappropriately attacking your opponent's credibility will harm *your* credibility, even if the attack succeeds. More importantly, it is essential that you focus on your goals. Do not let credibility contests become an un-goal. Your credibility is a tool for your use, not a goal to pursue. Winning credibility contests is likewise not a goal, but a means to an end.

## JUST SAY IT AIN'T SO

The first of the credibility arguments is "deny, deny, deny." Often featured in movies as a favorite of unscrupulous criminal defense lawyers, this argument essentially consists of repeating your point many times with great and unyielding conviction.

This sounds rather childish and silly, yet it can be effective—if you have the credibility to back it up. With sufficient credibility, almost anything you say can be credible so long as you can persuade your listener of your sincerity. And simple repetition can be persuasive evidence of sincerity.

This points us to the primary application of "deny, deny, deny," which is convincing your opponent of the sincerity and seriousness of your position—or opposition. When a four-year-old asks to watch TV and you say "No," the child is going to keep asking. You could say "No" to that request a dozen times without having any discernable effect on the child's determination.

In adult negotiations it works a little differently. After you reject a requested concession a few times, your opponent will begin to get the idea that this point is important to you—particularly if you tell them that this is important to you. If you declare a point a "non-starter" many people (myself included) will ignore you, and proceed as if the point is in fact open for discussion. After you have reiterated the non-starter-ness of that point a handful of times, however, even blockheads like me will get the point and start to believe that maybe this point really is not open for discussion. Simple repetition is powerful evidence of sincerity, and sometimes conveying sincerity is all you need to do.

But, as with all credibility arguments, there is a risk. The more times you repeat a position, the more credibility you have lined up behind that position—and your sincerity. If you suddenly give on this issue after a month of repeating that it was non-negotiable, then you just lost a fair amount of issue credibility, and your sincerity on other issues will be in doubt, possibly seriously so. All of a sudden all of your other "non-negotiable" positions reappear; they are now fair game once again.

## ELEMENTARY, MY DEAR WATSON

Another popular credibility argument, and one that often slips by unnoticed, is the "obvious" argument. The "obvious" argument is not really an argument at all, but simply a statement of fact without backup. Or, more specifically, a statement of fact without backup other than the claimant's big mountain of credibility. Whenever you hear someone say "Obviously, [...claim...]," they are really saying "trust me, because I have lots of credibility."

However, they are saying more, to those who listen. They are also saying "Ignore the man behind the curtain." Whenever you hear "obviously" (or any similar word or phrase, such as "of course" and "certainly"), your ears should perk up. "Obviously" is usually code for "I can't prove it." When faced with this statement, you should consider responding with a demand for explanation and support for the "obvious" fact. Even if the claim turns out to be true, you

> **Pro Tip:** You cannot bluff your way to credibility. Build credibility the hard way. And do so before you need it.

will often find that the claimant does not have handy evidence or support, and his failure to provide on-the-spot proof of his "obvious" fact will undermine his credibility. Much like the car dealer in Rule #3 ("Prepare; Then Prepare Some More"), you have rendered the truth irrelevant by exposing his lack of preparation.

Even if you do not openly challenge the statement at that time, you should make note of it, and then double-check the truth of the statement yourself—for a possible later challenge.

Why do people say "obviously" when things are not in fact obvious? Well, that is exactly *why* they say it is obvious. It is an attempt to bolster a statement without the fuss and difficulty of actually backing it up with real facts. The word "obvious" places your credibility behind the statement, and any challenge of the statement is a challenge to your credibility. If you have significant credibility this can be quite effective. "Obviously" is frequently a bluff, but it can be a powerful bluff. Calling this bluff can be dangerous.

Which in turn means that you should carefully consider the risks before challenging "obvious" statements. Unless you have some evidence that the statement is or might be incorrect, such a challenge essentially puts your credibility up against the credibility of the claimant. You just challenged your opponent to a credibility duel. If there are other participants in the exchange, they may have been persuaded by the initial claim of obviousness, and your challenge to the claim is therefore now also effectively a challenge to them. This raises the stakes. Do you want to raise the stakes?

As a result you will need to do better than merely challenge the statement: You now need to provide a counter-argument, or at least introduce a reasonable doubt. If the claimant says that something is obvious, and you simply challenge with "obvious how?" (or whatever) and the claimant can provide a quick explanation, you now look stupid for not understanding the obvious point. This will cost you credibility. If, on the other hand, your challenge includes a potential scenario for why the claim may not be so obvious, then you have won the exchange even if the claimant can respond sufficiently. Even if the claim is now true, it is no longer "obvious," and this will cost the claimant credibility. You have successfully challenged the obviousness of the statement, which can be as effective as challenging the statement itself.

Quite often, however, you will find that an educated challenge (You prepared for your negotiation and therefore fully understand all the issues, right? Your challenge is not just a gamble, right?) will be met with inability to defend the claim of obviousness. People claim something is obvious because they don't want to defend it, which usually means they cannot defend it. You will thereby gain substantial credibility at the expense of your opponent.

## BEEN THERE, DONE THAT

The arrogant and slightly educated cousin of "obvious" is "customary." A favorite of negotiators with substantial experience in a particular field, it goes like this: "Well, it is customary for the buyer to pay for the destination charge" or "I have been doing these deals for 15 years, and I have never seen that kind of termination fee." No justification is offered beyond a simple statement that "this is how it is done." Stack up a tall pile of credibility behind that statement, and it becomes a powerful argument. Your opponent has declared himself your superior, and placed you in a situation where any response you make will be discounted as the rant of a rookie. This is not merely a credibility argument, but a direct attack on *your* credibility. You must defend yourself.

If you believe you have more credibility than your opponent gives you credit for, you have the option of facing this challenge head on: "Well, I have bought many cars over the years, and I have never paid a destination charge," or "I have done eight of these deals in the last year, and half of them had this termination fee." This exchange just became a staring contest, fueled by credibility. Risky, but potentially effective in neutralizing this particular argument. It is important to note that to win this particular staring contest you do not need *more* credibility than your opponent—you only need enough credibility to show that you are in fact not an incompetent rookie, thereby defeating his claim that you do not know what you are talking about.

The subtly different alternate approach (and usually my preferred option) is to deflate the argument with facts and logic:

"That may or may not be true, but this deal is different, and the termination fee makes sense in *this* deal because...." The "customary" argument rests on an implication that you are incompetent and under-informed—it is fairly rare that past custom alone constitutes a substantive reason for continuing the custom. By demonstrating your understanding of the current transaction, including how it differs from prior deals, you have demonstrated that you are in fact neither incompetent nor under-informed, even if you do not have the same amount of direct experience as your opponent. This renders your opponent's statement irrelevant, and gains you credibility in the process— without the risk of a head-on credibility confrontation.

---

As a junior associate I was attending a negotiation session for a large power contract. A mid-level associate was lead negotiator for our side.

Every attorney on the other side was at least 10 years older than either of us.

At one stage, an attorney from the other side declared that our position on a particular issue was completely unacceptable, because it was contrary to every transaction she had worked on in her 20 years of practicing law.

The associate leading the talks for our side was accustomed to being underestimated and attacked, and she had little patience for it. Her response:

"That's great. I am sure you had fun working on all those deals. But unless those other deals were EXACTLY the same as this one, I just don't give a [expletive] what you bullied some incompetent lawyers into accepting ten years ago. Now let's get back to the present. Thank you."

---

Of course, that only works if you have followed Rule #3 ("Prepare; Then Prepare Some More") and are fully prepared. If you are not fully prepared, you will be unable to defend yourself against the "customary" argument. Follow Rule #3. Always follow Rule #3. Prepare; then prepare some more.

There are circumstances where the "customary" argument gets promoted from credibility challenge to actual substantive point. This occurs frequently when dealing with mid-level functionaries. It is often their goal/un-goal simply to not do anything out of the ordinary. Sometimes standing out from the crowd is a cliff all of its own, regardless of the substance of the issue. The same applies

> **Pro Tip:** There is a difference between the confidence you have in yourself and the confidence others have in you.

when dealing with corporate officers and directors, who can find shelter from their fiduciary obligations by doing something "customary."

When faced with this situation, when it is apparent that all your opponent wants is to get what is "market"—then informing him that your offer is indeed market/customary can be all the argument you need. In this context, "customary" is more of a reassurance than an attempt at persuasion. By taking the "market" deal, your opponent is comfortable that he will face no repercussions if the result is bad. All your opponent wants is to take the safe route. Help him.

## CALL IN THE CAVALRY

Sometimes you can artificially boost your credibility for certain arguments by leaning on a greater authority and borrowing their credibility: you bring an expert. An expert is someone generally acknowledged as having a massive issue credibility advantage on a particular subject. An environmental lawyer is an expert on environmental issues when in a group of non-environmental lawyers, but is not an expert (for purposes of this Rule) when in a group of other environmental lawyers. An environmental lawyer is not an expert unless the issue at hand is actually environmental law (or if he also happens to be expert on the current issue).

This massive issue credibility advantage essentially means that no one present can mount a credible argument against whatever the expert says. The word of an unopposed expert will be treated as fact, at least for the moment. Only another expert can argue against an expert. This makes experts powerful tools. If you can bring an expert to the table who will be unopposed, you will have an almost insurmountable advantage on that issue. By the same token, if your opponent has an expert, then you need one as well if you are to preserve the point. If your expert isn't handy at the moment you can declare the issue off the table until you can find an expert, but if you are unable to find an expert you will eventually be forced to cede the point to the unopposed expert.

> During negotiations I hardly ever mention anything from my own résumé. This type of bragging would not boost my credibility—quite the opposite.
>
> This social rule of modesty does not apply to third-party introductions, however. When introducing experts I make sure to do as much résumé-quoting as socially permissible. This is not for flattery: it establishes the credibility of my expert.
>
> One of my partners, for example, was involved with the drafting of the Internal Revenue Code. A simple mention of this (and I do always make sure to mention this) creates the instant presumption that he is *the* tax expert in the room.

When both sides have an expert on an issue, a battle of the titans ensues. The experts will have their own mini-negotiation, and if they reach agreement the rest of the group will follow. Should the experts fail to agree, however, the rest of the group, having witnessed the exchange, will find itself in a sort of jury role. The group will now essentially pick the winner of the expert debate, and this decision will be made primarily on the relative credibility of the experts—it has to be, since the group cannot legitimately evaluate the substantive discussion. As a result, you must choose your own expert not just on substance, but on presentation as well.

What this means for you as a lead negotiator is that unopposed experts are great, but if there is to be a rumble of the experts you should make sure that you have the better expert—and that means the expert who will likely have the most credibility *after* an expert exchange. If you have a truly powerful expert, you should wield her like a weapon of mass destruction, and find any excuse to bring her into the mix.

Negotiation is a social exercise, and credibility is a currency of social interaction. Use whatever currencies are at your disposal, specifically including credibility—yours and everyone else's.

# Rule Number 10

## Care

Caring is important. The subject of the negotiation is important to *someone;* otherwise you wouldn't be sitting there. Negotiation is serious business, so take it seriously.

## Care

You must care. If you are merely going through the motions, your opponent can tell. If you are treating it like a game, he can tell. Either way you have little chance of success. An argument without passion will almost certainly fail.

You must have commitment to the issue, and you must show that commitment. Lack of commitment is a weakness, and your opponent will exploit that weakness. Moreover, it will be difficult for you to sustain an argument that you do not care about.

Professional negotiators argue with passion, for they believe that their cause is righteous and their position correct. Arguing with passion does not mean being yelly or emotional; it means that you have some conviction in what you are saying.

## Prepare To Care

It is easy for me to simply declare that you must care about your positions and your arguments, but it is more difficult to actually achieve that caring. Yet the path to caring is the same path we have been on all along: Apply Rule #1 ("What Are You Trying To Achieve?")…and know your goals. Then apply Rule #3 ("Prepare; Then Prepare Some More")…and prepare. If you have thoroughly evaluated your

> **Pro Tip:** Do not confuse "caring" with "wild-eyed obsession." Maintain a calm, professional demeanor.

goals, and thoroughly prepared yourself by researching the facts and the law, and by practicing your arguments—well, it would take a cold soul *not* to care.

If you do not care, that usually means that you simply are not invested in the subject or position, and if you are not invested in the subject or position, that almost by definition means that you are not fully prepared. So prepare. Then care.

If you cannot make yourself believe in a variety of causes, you will have a difficult time as an attorney. If you truly cannot believe in a particular cause, then maybe you have the wrong cause—or the wrong job.

> When I started work with my first firm, one of my classmates was looking through the new matter list and noticed that our firm did some work for a tobacco company.
>
> He expressed his disgust to me, and told me that he would never work on a matter for a tobacco client, or on any matter for the benefit of tobacco companies.
>
> At the time, I thought he was being a little sanctimonious. In retrospect, however, it is clear that he would not have been able to represent a tobacco client's interests well, simply because of his inability to care about their goals.

## ONLY THE WEAK DO NOT CARE

Your opponent must also care about his cause to be effective. Don't assume that your opponent cares. Observe. If you spot indifference, this is a chink in his armor, a weakness. If your opponent does not care about his point or his argument, then he can be talked out of it. Indifference is a beacon, a target for you to focus on. Take ruthless advantage of this weakness.

When your opponent is an attorney or other representative you will occasionally notice that while she is trying hard to argue a point that is clearly of great interest to her client, she herself is less attached to the issue or argument. Better yet, you might see signs that the attorney actually agrees with your position, and is essentially looking for permission from her client to cede the point. Perhaps the lawyer glances over at the client as if seeking confirmation, or shuffles her papers, or weakly repeats lame arguments. These are signs of victory headed your way. When you spot these signs, don't interfere. You are winning. Don't screw it up by over-talking. Guide her towards surrender; you are now on her side. Gently feed her the ammunition she needs

> **Pro Tip:** Lawyers looking at their clients mid-sentence are asking approval or permission for something—usually the very thing they are saying.

to convince her client to concede. Halt any appearance of aggression or hostility. Remove un-goals that would keep your opponent in the fight. Make it a gentle landing. Offer an honorable surrender.

But don't confuse this impending surrender with simple weakness. Chase weakness. When your opponent is weak, attack that weakness. Lack of commitment, on the other hand, requires a gentle touch.

Watch for indicators of logic-induced apathy as well as original apathy. Even if your opponent believed in his argument at the outset, your logical counterargument might have dented his faith, and he is now looking for an excuse to ditch his position. Help him.

## DON'T CARE

Of equal importance to your commitment to the issue is your *lack* of commitment to the transaction. You must be willing—truly willing—to walk. If your minimum requirements are not met, you need to be able to just walk away. Over-commitment to the deal is even more transparent and exploitable than under-commitment to an issue. You will never win a negotiation if you are never prepared to walk. Your opponent won't even have to appease you if you are over-committed.

Getting the deal done is not a goal—to the contrary, it is an un-goal. Your goal is to get the deal done *on your terms.* Getting any old deal done is not the point of the exercise. If you honestly, truly, absolutely *must* get the deal done on whatever terms (this is very, very rare; there is almost always *some* alternative), then you had best pray that your opponent does not discover your predicament. If he does, most if not all of your leverage is gone and you will be forced to accept a bad deal. Now all you can do is hold individual issues hostage to try to stem the bleeding.

> I recall discussing associate salaries with another partner at my firm. Other firms were raising their salaries, and we were considering doing so as well.
>
> I asked this partner what he thought we ought to pay the associates, in light of the threat of a potential associate exodus. His response:
>
> "We ought to pay them just enough that we are indifferent whether they quit or not."

But overwhelmingly you will have the option to walk, and you should be prepared to do so. You have to be ready to walk and be happy about it, knowing that you made the right choice. You are not happy to have killed the deal; you are happy that you did not agree to a bad deal. It is normal to feel regret at a missed opportunity, but you must not let that regret tempt you into accepting an unacceptable deal.

Many confuse a willingness to walk with the willingness to issue ultimatums. Bad negotiators are forever issuing ultimatums. "If you don't agree to this, the deal is off...." or "There is no point to talking about anything else until you agree to our three main points...blah, blah, blah." These ultimatums are almost always empty threats. Ultimatum-threateners are usually bluffing. Good negotiators may identify an issue as a goal or a cliff—something they truly need—and will do so in no uncertain terms, but they will rarely threaten to terminate the discussion just because there is resistance to one of their main issues. When the time has come, good negotiators don't *threaten* to leave—they just leave.

I fundamentally ignore any ultimatums issued to me. I ignore them because they are irrelevant. I mark the identified issue as important, but "they might walk" is not a consideration when I am evaluating our positions. I am not trying to "call their bluff"—I *don't care* if they are bluffing. Ultimatums are just as irrelevant whether they are real or not.

---

When considering a car purchase I had determined the exact car I wanted, and the exact maximum price I was willing to pay. (Rule #3: "Prepare; Then Prepare Some More")

After some back and forth with the car dealer, his price was still above my limit. I informed him of my limit, and he told me he could not accommodate my price.

So I left.

Two weeks later I received a phone call from the dealer. They were now willing to accept my price.

I "won" by getting the car at my price; but I had already won by not being bullied into paying more than my limit. I did not walk out as a ploy—I simply cared more about my goals than about closing the sale. I was not anxiously waiting for his call, because I was comfortable with my decision to walk. The dealer's ultimatum failed for the same reason: I simply did not care.

---

I ignore ultimatums because I take Rule #1 seriously and have my goals in order. If the other side is unable or unwilling to agree to terms that are acceptable, then it is unimportant that they are walking, because *we* were going to walk anyway. Terms are either acceptable or unacceptable. Unacceptable terms attached to an ultimatum are still just that: unacceptable terms. The ultimatum changes nothing.

Your willingness to walk is also an effective defense against appeasement. You can only be appeased if you are afraid of the nuclear option. If you are indifferent about the nuclear option because you just don't care, then appeasement holds no power over you.

This special kind of indifference is an essential requirement for negotiation success, but do not confuse the willingness to walk with apathy. Not caring whether you walk is not the same as not caring about the issue. The first part of this Rule #10 ("Care") still applies, and you *must* care— just not so much that you are married to the deal and force yourself into abandoning your goals. You must care about the right things, and not care about the wrong things.

> **Pro Tip:** Sometimes quitting and getting fired are the same thing.

## Don't Take It Personally

Somewhere between the importance of caring and the importance of not caring lies the importance of caring just right, and maintaining a professional distance from the issues. During negotiations, a variety of issues, positions, arguments, and documents will be addressed, analyzed, dissected, and criticized. That includes *your* issues, positions, arguments, and documents. Your opponents will attempt to talk you away from your positions and attempt to change your documents. In the process of doing so, your documents will be criticized, your positions dissected, your arguments mocked.

You must rise above this.

These are not personal attacks—and even if they are, it does not matter. Protecting your ego is an un-goal. You must avoid this. Stay cool. So someone wants to spend thirty minutes demolishing your carefully prepared argument. Fine. This does not mean that you should get upset. Getting upset is not only not productive, but is actively counter-productive. You cannot take it personally. Your opponent is attempting to reach his goals. This is not about you. Do not make it about you. Sure, you can express righteous indignation to actual personal attacks, but do not let them get to you, and do not reinterpret a simple argument into a personal attack that probably is not there. Things will get heated from time to time during negotiations, sure, and you have to cope with that. If every pointed statement knocks you off track, you will never stay on track.

---

In a fairly complex transaction I was faced with opposing counsel who took offense at...everything. He should have known better, as he was a partner at a major law firm, but he apparently did not.

Every argument was interpreted as an underhanded attempt at sneaking something by him; every suggested revision was a slight on his drafting skills.

During the first several sessions, we spent more time pacifying this lawyer than we did actually discussing issues. After that, when possible sessions were conducted without him. How? We scheduled meetings without *me*, thereby precluding him from attending (due to ethical rules and social niceties). Fortunately our client was sophisticated, so my advice for me not to participate worked.

Not surprisingly, that lawyer was not retained by the other side for their future transactions.

---

Even statements that sound distinctly like personal attacks often are not. Some people lack fully-functioning social filters (yours truly among them), and will say things that strike others as rude and even insulting, yet go on as if they had said nothing other than a friendly "Hello." These folks aren't saying anything inappropriate (at least to their way of thinking); they just accept blunt talk as normal and certainly as nothing personal. Perhaps surprisingly, these "unfiltered" types are present in large numbers among the ranks of professional negotiators. Learn to identify them, and treat what they say as water off a duck's back.

> **Pro Tip:** You defend against personal attacks by your actions, not by your words.

And, frankly, even if there are intentional personal attacks (which unfortunately will occur from time to time), you need to stay cool—or terminate the discussion. A negotiation full of personal insults is difficult and probably won't get you very far, but getting into a shouting match is guaranteed not to get you anywhere at all.

Ignoring the un-goal of retaliation does not mean that you should ignore the personal attack. You need to defend yourself: Not reacting *at all* to direct personal insults can make you look weak and cause you to lose credibility. But do not retaliate. Address any direct accusations as required, and declare other personal attacks non-productive and irrelevant. Do not elevate personal attacks to anything more than a distraction. Do not engage in an *ad hominem* battle, but instead move on to do something productive. Spending an unnecessary amount of time discussing personal attacks is almost as counterproductive as engaging in them yourself.

> While working on a particularly adversarial transaction I was faced with an unscrupulous (non-attorney) opponent who, during a negotiation session, circulated a "memo" to the entire group (including me). This memo was little more than a direct attack on my character and professional abilities.
>
> I chose to disregard the libelous memo and proceed as if nothing had happened, mostly because I was shell-shocked. My failure to defend myself shook my client's confidence in me, very much to my immediate detriment.

Rule #1 ("What Are You Trying To Achieve?") trumps all. Work towards the goals, away from the cliffs, while pointedly ignoring the un-goals.

The goals are the goals, and personal insults—perceived or real—are not relevant to your goals. Personal insults are your opponent's way of dangling an un-goal in front of your face. Do not take the bait.

# Rule Number 11

## Understand The Environment

All negotiations are different. This is obvious in some ways, but not so obvious in other, equally important ways. Yes, the contract (or whatever) being negotiated is different. Yes, the facts are different. Yes, each transaction is different. Yes, the issues are different.

Whatever. That's easy.

Where you really have to pay attention is with the environmental variables. I am using "environmental" in a broad sense here, to mean *all* external factors that could affect the negotiations. This is a uselessly broad description, of course, but the subject areas that merit attention include:

- Format: Is it a meeting, a conference call, an email exchange?
- What are the time constraints?
- Is there a preset issues list or agenda?
- Is it a planned or *ad hoc* session?
- Is it even an official "negotiation," or just an informal chat?
- Are there formal procedural rules that apply?
- Is there a dress code?
- Who is hosting? Who is visiting, and from where?
- Who is attending? Are there important people not attending?
- Is there somebody unexpected on the call?
- Who is sitting where?
- What is the weather? (No, I am not kidding.)
- Are there refreshments available?
- Are there convenient break-out spaces available?
- Which side is expected to start the discussion?

Some of these topics may appear absurd or irrelevant, or just petty. They may in fact be both absurd and petty, but they are only rarely irrelevant. These topics (and many more) are important, and you need to understand them and how they interact with your negotiations. Because interact they will, whether you understand them or not.

## Planes, Trains, and Automobiles

The first item on that list is relatively easy. Clearly (I hope) it is important to know whether the negotiation session will be on the phone or in person. Less clear, perhaps, is the extent of the resulting effects.

If the session is on the phone, you may be seated at your desk in front of your computer, having full and easy access to all your files, documents, and correspondence. If you are meeting in person, on the other hand, you may be limited to whatever documents you can carry, especially if the meeting is away from your office. In Rule #3 ("Prepare; Then Prepare Some More"), I mentioned how some negotiations are like open-book exams and others are like closed-book exams. Here is a perfect example. This does not mean that you can prepare *less* for a conference call just because you have unlimited access to information; it just means that you have to prepare *correctly* for that session format.

> A senior partner I worked with for many years took meetings *very* seriously. Before meetings he would often send an associate into the conference room to (surreptitiously) identify who was there and where they were sitting. He did not want any surprises when he entered the room.

But wait…there's more. On a conference call you cannot see each other. This means that you can make funny faces and obscene gestures all you want, but it also means that you cannot use non-verbal communications in your favor. You now have to shape your conversation accordingly. That sarcastic joke that is such a hit over drinks? On the phone, opposing counsel cannot see your sardonic smile and could be offended. And, of course, you might not be able to tell whether or not he *is* offended, because you can't see him either.

On a conference call you cannot lean over and whisper in your client's ear. If you need a sidebar, you will have to set up a separate line, or manage the exchange by email. This makes it difficult to have quick side discussions—but email can also make those side discussions invisible, almost.

The environmental differences between a phone call and an in-person meeting make up a long list. Many, or all, of these differences can have an impact on your negotiation, and you need to understand and consider those differences.

And that's just telephone versus in-person. Written negotiations are also common. When expressing your opinions on paper (or virtual paper), you have to adapt your tone. You also have to consider that you are now creating a record that can (and often will) come back to haunt you. And if the written negotiation is simply a marked-up document, you have to decide whether (and how) to include reasoning for your suggested revisions, or to let the mark-up speak for itself. There is usually not a single correct answer, but ignoring such a factor is nearly always the wrong answer.

And we are still on the first item on my partial list of environmental variables.

Time constraints are equally important, and interact with the session format. There are always time constraints—no one has infinite time. Sometimes the constraints are hard, sometimes soft. Sometimes there is enough time, sometimes not. You need to know, and you need to plan accordingly.

> **Pro Tip:** Always know what time it is.

Opposing counsel has to leave for the airport by 3:45? Best get all the "legal" issues resolved by then, even if the non-legal folks continue the discussion after her departure. You have a one-hour conference call, but enough issues for three hours? How will this affect your ability to resolve issues in your favor?

Is this a large meeting, with a bunch of people traveling and a set agenda? Now you *really* need to prepare; then prepare some more. If you thought you had to prepare for a "regular" negotiation, that was nothing: For this kind of negotiation you really *really* have to prepare. Why? Because these meetings are rare, expensive, difficult to arrange, and usually more consequential. You cannot expect to punt issues from this meeting. All the participants will expect significant progress and definable results. You will usually not be able to go off and research an issue in the middle of the meeting. (Unless you have helpers on standby. Therefore you should try to have helpers on standby).

A random unplanned phone call, on the other hand, allows you a fair amount of discretion to reserve on issues and limit your conclusions. That doesn't mean you shouldn't prepare, of course, but the environmental factors now provide you some "outs" that were not available in the big meeting.

## RULES, SCHMULES?

There will be rules. There are always rules. And you absolutely, unconditionally, *must* understand the rules. It is perhaps painfully obvious that you should know the rules of procedure and evidence when in litigation (which, of course, is the ugly country cousin of civilized negotiation), but there are plenty of non-litigation forums with rules as well.

In certain administrative proceedings, for instance, the "arbitrator" and your opponent may be one and the same, which simply makes this a negotiation—yet with semi-rigid rules of procedure that apply. The same applies for almost any government interaction. There will be rules. Filing complex permit applications includes providing carefully selected information, carefully and artfully phrased to sway the evaluation of the application in your favor. That's a negotiation, and not only do you need to understand the substantive law regarding the permit, but—equally importantly—you must understand the procedures. What information will be considered, and what will not? Can you contact the government official directly, or is that against the rules? Are there informal rules? Informal rules can often be as significant as formal, written rules—even beyond mere social custom—and you must know these informal rules as well as the official rules.

This analysis also applies to formal Requests For Proposals (RFPs) in the private sector. Large RFPs often have elaborate rules for how to submit bids: What to include, what not to include, whom to talk to and when, and so forth. You have to comply with all of these procedural rules while at the same time being persuasive in your written submittal. Failure to understand the rules will at best put you at a disadvantage against those who paid more attention and prepared more, and at worst will simply get your submittal disqualified. You must, must, *must* understand the rules.

We can take these principles beyond obvious negotiation formats. Perhaps you are making a public presentation regarding your client's project. Don't kid yourself: You are negotiating…with your audience, with the public, with decision-makers, with whomever, but you are doing so in a highly constrained format. You may have 35 minutes for your prepared presentation, and then 15 minutes to answer questions fielded from the floor. Those are the rules, and you must abide by them.

You must also be careful how your message to one audience can cause inadvertent problems with another audience—for example, commissioners versus the public, or a client versus the opponent. You must therefore precisely tailor your responses based on, yes, those formal *and* informal rules. Failure to understand these rules—all of them—and failure to adapt to the circumstances will severely handicap your effectiveness.

## TAKE OFF YOUR SHOES AND BOW

Up to this point, these are just "hard" rules. The hard rules are drastically outweighed by the soft rules of human interaction. Are you wearing jeans, and everyone else is in a suit? Don't think it will go unnoticed. It is easy to think of social *faux pas* as things that were important for Americans doing business in Japan in the

1980s (bow, take your shoes off, etc.), but the truth is that every society has social rules and expectations, including ours. We just don't notice the ones we grew up with, because they are natural to us. We also don't realize just how important these rules are—until we see one violated. We might be more forgiving of a foreign counterpart who commits a social *faux pas;* we are less inclined to be forgiving of a violator who "should know better."

> As a first-year associate I accompanied a partner on a multi-day trip for the negotiation of a potential acquisition.
>
> The discussions did not go well. The first day was spent mostly in a stalemate over a single issue, and ended with the parties in stark disagreement, the deal dead, and the next day's session cancelled.
>
> To my surprise the partner, who was not known as a social butterfly, invited opposing counsel out for a drink.
>
> When I quizzed him on why we were having drinks instead of returning home, he smiled:
>
> "Oh, the deal isn't dead. We will continue negotiating over drinks this afternoon. I expect we will close this deal by April."
>
> Which we did.

Well, in a negotiation context the rules might be shifted a little. Behaving how your mother told you to will get you far, but this is about more than just being polite and well-behaved. Nothing from your childhood would inform you about the expected seating arrangement in a conference room, for instance, or the correct amount of small talk at the beginning of a conference call, yet these are rules you must learn and rules you must follow.

The real lesson here is that those rules vary, and they may be subtly different from time to time, or place to place. The cultural differences between Milwaukee and San Diego may not be as significant as those between New York and Tokyo, but it would be a mistake to pretend there are no differences at all, or that those differences will not affect the negotiations. You absolutely must be socially aware. If this is difficult for you, try harder. This is not optional. Rule #4 ("It's All About Credibility") tells you to maintain social credibility, but Rule #4 doesn't work if you aren't paying attention.

The applicable rules will also vary depending on who is in the meeting. Different rules apply to meetings with CEOs than to meetings with sales managers—and even meetings with participants from different age groups. Nothing can be ignored.

And, of course, all of those other issues listed above (and others) will determine which social rules are in play. Heavy time constraint? Maybe keep the chit-chat to a bare minimum. Long meeting? Breaks are expected. Water. Food. And so forth— and thinking about these beforehand will almost certainly help with a better meeting, logistically, which will almost certainly help with a better meeting, substantively.

**Pro Tip:** Pay attention. To everything.

There is no way to predict the many permutations of social rules that come into play during negotiations, any more than I can possibly list all of the environmental factors that you must consider for a negotiation. The central point is that you absolutely cannot view your negotiation as an isolated issues list living in a bubble of thought and ideas. The real world can and will come crashing in on your negotiation party to mess with your plans.

Accept it, and prepare accordingly.

# Rule Number 12

## Control The Environment

This Rule is easy. Here…I will summarize it for you: Take all those things from Rule #11 ("Understand The Environment") and manipulate them to your advantage. There, done.

Easy and obvious? Yes and no.

Yes, understanding the environment is important. But why stop there? Many of the variables described in Rule #11 can be planned around, or even affirmatively controlled. Why leave things to chance?

Conference call or in-person meeting? That decision doesn't make itself. *Someone* decides that it should be one or the other, and that someone might as well be you.

Do you have a hypnotic phone voice, but an annoying habit of frequently scratching yourself? You might want to push for the conference call. Do you have a steely gaze but a squeaky voice? An in-person meeting might be the better arrangement.

Okay, so those two examples are a bit goofy, but the point stands. Only rarely will you be truly neutral as to whether there is a conference call, a meeting, or just an exchange of drafts. One of those is almost certainly better for you than the other—so make it happen! Don't wait for somebody else to randomly (or not-so-randomly) choose the format. *You* decide the format, and you decide the format that is best for *you*.

---

The senior partner I described in Rule #11 preferred to do more than simply see who was sitting where.

Before meetings he liked to visit the conference room and plan out a seating chart. He would determine where he would sit, where he wanted the various client personnel to sit, and where he wanted the other side to sit. If needed, we would rearrange chairs to make sure people had little choice but to unwittingly comply with his plan.

The same goes for timing. Somebody has to decide when to negotiate; it might as well be you. Controlling the schedule gives you power. Use it. Location. Agenda. Attendees. Use them all. Don't let chance—or worse, your adversary—dictate the circumstances of your negotiation. The environment is there for the using. Use it.

## RING RING

Your phone rings. The caller ID shows that it is opposing counsel, and you figure he is probably calling about the extension term pricing in the agreement you are working on. You reach for the phone.

Stop!

Not so fast.

Why are you answering the phone? He is calling to negotiate. When you pick up the phone, you will instantly be negotiating. Every interaction with opposing counsel is part of the negotiation. Are you prepared to negotiate extension term pricing? Really prepared? Rule #3 prepared? Are you Rule #3 prepared *right now?* Are you doing something else that is distracting you at that moment, like working on another deal? Are you in the zone for extension term pricing, or are you mentally still on that other deal?

If you are not fully and properly prepared, why would you answer the phone? Let the call go to voicemail instead. Finish your other work. Go to the bathroom. Collect your notes and your thoughts, plan out your arguments, give yourself a pep talk, and then, when you are ready, truly ready, *then* you call him back to negotiate. You will negotiate when *you* are good and ready, thank you very much, not when *he* feels like negotiating. You can and should control your environment to your liking.

> **Pro Tip:** Never make a telephone call unless you know what you are going to say.

Do not let opposing counsel bully you into negotiating when you are not ready.

Generally speaking, the person placing an unannounced phone call has an advantage. She knows it is negotiating time, she is prepared, and she is mentally ready. The recipient of the unannounced call, on the other hand, is almost by definition never fully prepared or mentally ready. Don't let opposing counsel put you at a disadvantage with something as simple as a phone call.

Of course, this does not mean that you should never answer the phone. Social rules and credibility concerns still apply, and the deal will never get done if nobody answers phone calls. What it does mean is that you cannot treat that phone call as "just a phone call." That phone call is part of the negotiation, and you need to act accordingly.

Maybe you weren't planning on screening your calls, but opposing counsel happened to call when you were still putting together your issues list, and not quite ready for a discussion. In this situation picking up the phone is not merely surrendering a minor tactical advantage, but actively placing yourself in a situation where you are about to enter a negotiation unprepared.

If you nevertheless feel socially obligated to answer the phone, do so only to listen. Encourage him to set out the issues he's calling about, and then tell him something along the lines of "That's great, thanks for calling. This isn't a good time to talk. Can I get back to you on Tuesday morning." Applied with care, this approach will allow you to find out something about his position, gain some time to consider before responding—all without violating social convention. Just because you picked up the phone does not obligate you to engage.

Frankly, it usually isn't the end of the world if you pick up that phone call, and as you gain experience you will be better at switching gears on the fly. The underlying principle is important, however: You fundamentally want to be the one to dictate the circumstances of the negotiation, and you specifically do not want to let others dictate those circumstances to your detriment. You also fundamentally want to not only observe and adapt to the environment, but affirmatively shape it your advantage. The ringing telephone is only a single example. You must apply this principle to your entire environment, not just caller ID.

## BE THE RINGMASTER

Negotiations do not happen in a vacuum, and it is foolish to ignore opportunities to bend the environment in your favor. The point here is not to expend vast amounts of energy manipulating seating charts instead of preparing on the issues. The point here is that most environment-shaping requires relatively little effort; it mainly requires awareness. If you fully apply Rule #11 ("Understand The Environment"), this Rule will follow. This Rule requires that you understand the effects of environmental factors and make the conscious decision not to be a passive participant in that environment. Be the master of your own destiny.

> **Pro Tip:** Attorneys are bound by rules of legal ethics: rules for you to follow, but also for you to use.

---

For several years I worked with a partner who paid close attention to food during negotiations. He would go to great lengths to identify the best restaurants for post-session dinners, and took equal care when selecting the menu for conference room catering.

For veteran negotiators, conference room lunches start looking the same—but not when *this* partner was in charge. Even the most jaded banker took note of the excellent food...served with proper plates and silverware, of course.

After extended sessions, it was not uncommon for opposing parties to be friendlier with my partner than with their own attorneys.

---

As with phone calls, so also with procedural rules. If you are negotiating in a structured environment, do not just understand and obey the rules, but affirmatively *use* the rules. If (for whatever reason) Robert's Rules of Order are in effect during your session, then by all means make points of order and objections as to form. Make sure your opponent states her response in the form of a question. Whatever. While always watching your social *faux pas* meter, of course, you should use these rules. Simply following the rules like a polite little child will not suffice. Grab a hold of those rules and swing them like a club to smite your adversaries.

Social conventions as well: Use them. If you understand these conventions, you know when and how people are expected to speak. Complying with those conventions yourself is easy—now go and place your opponent in a position where she cannot speak without being rude. Make her choose between the issue and her credibility. Or do the opposite: Go out of your way to help your opponent get her point

> **Pro Tip:** Consider scheduling conference calls early in the day, so that you can distribute notes or documents the same day—thereby increasing your credibility (and placing pressure on the other side).

across, thereby manipulating the situation to gain credibility (and building rapport with opposing counsel). Social rules can be used to create goodwill as well as to tip the issues.

Rules are not mere restrictions. They are also tools. Use them.

Ditto for other constraints. Choose the conference room that best suits you. Do you think it is an accident that interrogations frequently take place in unpleasant, windowless rooms? Or that law firms showcase their fabulous conference centers, with views that stretch far

> **Pro Tip:** A simple smile (or frown) can change the mood of the room and the direction of the negotiations.

beyond the city into the suburban distance? The room is a player in any negotiation. It quite literally surrounds you.

Don't leave it to chance. Don't leave anything to chance.

Is there limited time for the parties to reach an agreement? Is someone heading to the airport in an hour? If so, you have to pretend you are a football coach at the end of the game. You either accelerate the process or slow it down, depending on which tempo will favor you. Don't let the other side dictate the tempo. And whether fast or slow, you need to manage the agenda as well. If there is not enough time to cover all the issues, you need to make sure that *your* issues get covered, while the issues that you do not want to discuss get pushed aside.

> **Pro Tip:** Arrive early for the meeting. Or on time. Or late. Whatever—but do it *on purpose.*

This is also an excellent time to offer tempting compromise solutions. Much real estate has been sold by clever brokers who simply understood the occasional inability of otherwise intelligent people to think clearly when the clock is ticking. Your opponents' time constraints are not *your* problem. Let them stress. You. Stay. Calm.

> **Pro Tip:** Eat well before an extended session. Let everyone else get antsy as lunch-time comes and goes.

As with everything else, social rules apply. You cannot rudely ignore your opponents' flight times, and any manipulation must be subtle, but nor can you afford to ignore the opportunity.

If you look, you can see environmental manipulation all around you. Witness the strange mating ritual that happens before every business dinner (and many social dinners), where diners stand behind chairs, gently jockeying for position to get the preferred seat while dearly holding on to their social credibility. Notice how the senior partner always seems to end up sitting next to the CEO. Coincidence? Of course not.

> **Pro Tip:** I like to sit with my back to the window during meetings—less glare, no distracting views.

These and a thousand other environmental variables are there for your use. Mostly they are little things and may not appear worth the effort, but the world is made of little things. Moreover, many of your opponents will understand and use the environment too, con-

sciously or subconsciously. If you find yourself constantly flatfoot-
ed, seemingly always rushed or unprepared, or sitting in the wrong
place and having a hard time getting a word in—well, it is possible
that you are inept, but maybe, just maybe, you are being forced into
a manipulated environment. And you didn't even notice.

# Rule Number 13
## Understand The People—
## Including Yourself

The weather, the seating chart, the time of day—those are all great, and certainly worthy of your attention, but there is one environmental factor that is far more important than all of those: the people.

Negotiation is ultimately a social exercise, and it is the interaction among the human participants that determines the outcome. Yes, the issues and the goals are important, but without an understanding of the human element you are lost.

---

As a mid-level associate I was negotiating a loan agreement, where my client was the borrower.

The bank was taking a hard line (as banks tend to do), and we were stuck on a single point relating to my client's use of funds for capital improvements. We were otherwise ready to go, but we could not get past this last point.

I was getting ready to recommend capitulation, but when I discussed the situation with my supervising partner, he told me to sit tight. He was confident the bank would cave soon.

When I asked him how he could be so sure, he answered: "Today is March 27. Bill (the banker) wants to book this loan before the end of the quarter. Bill has had a slow quarter, and he needs this loan to close or he isn't getting his bonus. Just wait—he will give."

And so it came to pass.

---

You, however, need to understand not just the "human element" in a philosophical fashion, but specifically the human element with regard to *these* people. The people at the table; the people on the phone; the people behind the keyboard. They are not abstractions or theoretical "people." They are human individuals.

You cannot address the issues removed from them. You will not be able to properly apply either Rule #4 ("It's All About Credibility") or Rule #9 ("Bring Credibility To The Table") to establish and use credibility unless you do so in the context of the specific individuals involved.

## KNOW YOUR ENEMY

There are distinct groups of people involved in the process. You must understand each of them. The first, and most obvious, group or person to understand is your opponent. Yes, you need to understand what he is trying to achieve, you need to list out his goals and un-goals—but that isn't enough. He is still a human being, and that humanity will impact the negotiation.

What is your opponent's limit of authority? Are you negotiating with the principal decision-maker, or the second-in-command who has to go to the back room to get the "approval of the manager?" If the lead negotiator on the other side is not the decision-maker, is the decision-maker in the room or on the phone? Is your opponent fresh out of school, or a grizzled veteran? What is his temperament? Did you and he go to the same college or law school? What is his favorite baseball team?

> **Pro Tip:** Everyone has a boss. *Everyone.*

Who is the lead negotiator? Who are the advisors? The guy you thought was the lead negotiator just sat down at the end of the table, but who is that sitting next to the CFO? How experienced is he on the specific subject matter? Does he like taking charge, or does he like observing? Is he a boss, or a consigliere?

What are the *personal* motivations of your opponent? Are his goals at odds with his client's goals? Is he up for partner this year? Is it dinnertime? Are there personal un-goals you can exploit? Is his wife about to go into labor, at which point he goes away and you have to deal with his replacement? Do you know who that replacement is, and is she better or worse to deal with than your current counterpart?

Who is his boss? Is the boss present? Is the boss showing up later? What is the nature of your opponent's job and company? Negotiating with representatives of utilities or government, for instance, can be challenging because they have excellent job security and fixed pay. As a result they often truly "Don't Care" on an individual level.

> **Pro Tip:** The testier you were with the subordinate, the nicer you should be with the boss.

You have already identified your goals and your opponent's goals, but does *he* have a good grasp of his own goals? What does he think *your* goals are?

Much of this you cannot know prior to negotiations, so you must observe. Watch the interpersonal dynamics of the other team. Look to see if your salesman is checking his watch. Take advantage of small talk at the beginning of the session and during breaks.

> **Pro Tip:** "Good cop, bad cop" really works. Seriously.

There is also information that can be gleaned ahead of a session. Computers are wonderful things, and the internet places immense information at your fingertips. Use it. Research your opponents. Research the company, but also the individuals. Read the online bios, look at the corporate chart, review the news stories.

Don't go in blind.

## KNOW YOUR FRIENDS

Once you have evaluated your opponent, you must evaluate your side of the table: your client and your colleagues. Is your client a hardass, or likely to surrender at the first sign of resistance? Does she have outside obligations coloring her priorities? Will she take or ignore your advice? Can she sit still without talking, or does she tend to blurt things out? Client management is an essential skill for any attorney, and it is particularly important during negotiations. You cannot manage your client if you do not understand your client.

Are your colleagues as prepared as you are? You brought your ERISA expert. How does he stack up against the other side's ERISA expert? Is he an asset or will he be a liability?

> A utility client I worked with regularly was extraordinarily patient. If the other side did not initially agree to our terms, we would simply wait until they did.

How prepared is your team? Did you have enough pre-negotiation discussions about goals and priorities? Is there a set strategy for presenting your demands and responding to theirs, or will the presentation be *ad hoc?* Is the extent of your authority clear, or do you expect frequent side-bars to discuss details?

> I was negotiating a construction contract with a construction company. I had worked up an issues and positions list with my client in advance. We had everything planned out.
>
> Or so I thought.
>
> My client had a past as a contractor. Several times during the negotiation session, when I pressed hard on a point, he would loudly and publicly declare that "as a contractor himself" he had sympathy with the other side, and that I was being unreasonable. Opposing counsel, a student of Rule #6 ("Sit Down And Shut Up"), did not disagree.
>
> The resulting contract was not favorable to my former-contractor client.

## SOMETIMES IT *IS* ABOUT YOU

Lastly, after you have evaluated your opponent and your team, you have to make the most important evaluation of all: yourself.

The time for pep-talks was an hour ago. This is the time for brutal honesty. Just how prepared are you…really? What are the gaps in your knowledge that you must avoid? What are your own outside motivations that are lingering un-goals, distracting you from your task?

---

My client was party to a consulting agreement, and the relationship was going sour.

We approached the other side with some contract modifications to improve the situation. They came back with a rather obnoxious counter-proposal, which would drastically reduce my client's profit.

My client was deeply personally vested in the transaction. She took great offense to the offer, and wanted to terminate the agreement and/or sue immediately. To that effect she composed an email to the other side that clearly and graphically stated her views.

She (wisely) showed me the draft email. I suggested that she not send it quite yet, and instead sleep on it over the weekend. The following Monday she was ready to discuss a less incendiary response.

---

Are you nervous? Confident? Tired, anxious, hungry? Do you need to go to the bathroom? Are *you* about to go into labor?

**Pro Tip:** If you are nervous, acknowledge this. Then give yourself an extra pep-talk and forge ahead anyway.

What is your appearance, your demeanor? How will you be perceived by opposing counsel or your client? Will either judge you too young, too inexperienced, or do you have the ability to instill confidence? Do you leap into conversation with strangers, or do you have a tendency to be stand-offish in a social setting? Be honest. This is not bragging time; this is honest-assessment time. Forget how prepared you are for a moment: Do you *look* prepared, or do you look disorganized and distracted?

Do you have a hypnotic voice, or a squeaky voice? Do you have a steely gaze, or an annoying habit of frequently scratching yourself? Does the meeting format play to your strengths or to your weaknesses?

Will your gender or ethnicity be an issue to anyone in the room? If so, how? Can you mitigate the effects—or use them to your advantage? Everything is fair game and must be assessed honestly, because the effects will be there whether or not they are appropriate, or even legal. Ignore them at your peril.

> I worked with a foreign-born associate who spoke flawless, accent-free English.
>
> Yet, somehow, whenever there was social benefit in revealing her origins, a subtle but unmistakable trace of an accent would suddenly appear.

As with the other environmental Rules, the point here is not to turn you into some obsessive micromanaging control freak, but simply to make you aware, and to encourage you to take the time— *consciously* take the time—to evaluate the situation and the people in that situation…especially yourself. Evaluating people does not have to take a lot of time, but you must make the mental effort.

You spent a lot of time preparing on the issues, and it is easy to fall into the trap of thinking that issues are everything. Certainly it is true that the issues and the substance are extremely important, but negotiation is ultimately a *social* exercise among *humans*. The participants in this drill are not computers exchanging points of logic. To be successful you absolutely must understand the human element.

# Rule Number 14

## Be Alpha

Negotiation is the art of convincing somebody that they are wrong and you are right; it is the art of convincing somebody to give you their stuff while giving them less in return; it is the art of leaving the room with more than you had when you entered.

### Stand Up And Be Counted

This requires strength. More specifically, it requires the absence of weakness. If you are to be a successful negotiator you need to be able to stand up (literally or metaphorically) and be heard. You need to be able to make everybody listen to YOU, even in a crowded room. You need for people to take you seriously, even if you have not yet had an opportunity to build credibility. You need a presence and an air of authority.

You need to be Alpha.

In a different time I might have written that you need to be an "Alpha Male," but there is no gender requirement for Alpha-ness. The concept holds, however, and Alpha (Male/Female) is what you need to be. You need to be top dog, boss of the room, head honcho, leader of the pack. You need to be *in charge.*

If you are the carrier of the briefcase, you are doomed to fail as a negotiator. If you are the quiet mouse in the corner, politely waiting your turn to speak, only to timidly offer your opinion, nobody will pay attention or take you seriously. It won't matter whether your point is valid; they already moved on to the next speaker. Wallflowers win no debates.

You need to take charge. You need to be confident and comfortable in your skin as well as in the moment, and you need to *exude* that confidence and comfort.

Alphas get to set the schedule and direct the agenda. Alphas run the discussion and wield significant authority in determining the tone and feel of the negotiation session. If you are Alpha, then it is *your* meeting. Rule #12 ("Control The Environment") is the Alpha's playground. Do not surrender this easily.

> During my first summer in law school I volunteered with a welfare law clinic. My job consisted largely of negotiating (begging) with agency officials for welfare benefits to which my clients were entitled. Occasionally there were administrative hearings, which were essentially semi-formal negotiations/trials.
>
> During my first such hearing, I politely sat and listened while the agency bureaucrat argued his position to the arbitrator. And I waited, and I waited. I figured that eventually they would tell me it was my turn.
>
> More honestly, I was nervous, uncertain, and generally terrified. Thankfully, my supervisor (a crusty old law professor) had accompanied me for my first hearing. After watching the proceedings for a while, he unceremoniously elbowed me in the ribs and gruffly told me, "Say something!"

There can be—and usually are, in a business negotiation—multiple Alphas. You do not need to be the *only* Alpha in the room; you just need to be Alpha enough to stand your ground when the other Alphas come charging at you.

Importantly, you do not need to be loud, or an ass—or a loud ass—to be Alpha. All too often people think that the way to establish one's Alphaness is to just speak louder than everyone else in the room, or worse, insult and belittle everyone else.

> **Pro Tip:** An Alpha greets obstacles not with fear but annoyance.

There are many ways to be Alpha. Being loud is one of those ways, but certainly not the only way (and probably not the best way). Many fine Alphas are the "strong, silent type," who speak rarely and softly, but whose words prompt immediate attention. "Alpha," for our purposes, does not even have to mean that you are a "Type A personality." Alphaness for negotiations is determined situationally. You don't have to be Alpha all the time: You have to be able to turn the Alpha on when needed. If, for example, you are the expert on a specific issue vital to the negotiation, when attention turns to that point you need to be ready. You need to be *ready* to be Alpha.

> I have a friend who is a law enforcement officer. In his natural state he speaks softly, looks harmless, and usually sports a goofy grin.
>
> While vacationing together with our families we were set upon by a couple of thugs in a restaurant parking lot. After the initial verbal threats and posturing, one of the thugs advanced towards me with clear violent intent.
>
> Without missing a beat my harmless-looking friend transformed himself into an imposing presence. He stepped in front of the advancing thug, pointed a finger at him, gave him a stern look, and barked at him to back down.
>
> The thugs ran to their car and drove off, and my friend flashed me a goofy grin as we continued our family vacation.
>
> Alpha. On command.

Being Alpha is not a personality trait, but a skill.

Some people let Alphaness take over, and when two of these people are in the room together, an otherwise productive negotiation session can quickly deteriorate into a pissing contest between two overblown egos. Do not let your Alphaness become an ungoal. Being Alpha is a tool, like any other tool at your disposal. An important tool, to be sure, but a tool nonetheless.

While "Alpha" is often taken to be synonymous with "leader," this need not be so. Being Alpha does not mean that you have to *always* be in charge and run the show. It is perfectly normal for the client to take the lead during negotiations, and you serve as the trusted advisor. You will offer opinions when appropriate, either to the client or to the other side, but you are not the director—or the dictator. Not only is it possible to fill this role while being Alpha, but being Alpha is just as necessary for the advisor as for the lead negotiator. Being a trusted advisor requires the same aura of confidence as it does to be the lead. The leader-advisor relationship is among the most important in all of leadership—not to mention, in all of lawyerdom.

Unsurprisingly, being Alpha interacts closely with personal credibility. But they are not the same. Sometimes pursuing one conflicts with the other: being obnoxious and rude may establish you as the top dog in the room, but the damage to your credibility will cripple you as a negotiator. On the

> **Pro Tip:** Faking Alpha can help make you Alpha.

other hand, having lots of credibility almost automatically makes you Alpha. Almost. The problem for beginning negotiators, of course, is that you *don't* have lots of credibility; you hardly have any at all. You will have to establish your Alphaness by other means.

## SEEK THE MAGIC

How then to be Alpha? Well, that is indeed the million dollar question. If it were easy, we would all do it, but the reality is that many never quite figure it out. Yet this is something you *must* master. Your success as a negotiator will depend in no small part on your ability to be Alpha.

At the same time, it is not witchcraft. There is no shortage of Alphas in the world. Plenty of people figure it out. Here are some pointers.

As mentioned earlier, having credibility helps greatly, and implied credibility works too. Your opponents will observe the interactions among your team. Your opponents will decide who is the leader of your pack not based on who *says* he is the leader, but

> **Pro Tip:** If you cannot spot the leader in a room, there is a vacuum for you to fill.

based on who the members of your team *treat* as the leader. If you

have the respect of your own team—your client, your colleagues—
then that respect (that credibility) will help establish you as Alpha.

On the other hand, if you are the guy carrying the boss' documents and getting coffee, you have pretty much been established as
*not* Alpha.

This, of course, is one reason why some negotiators (and other
people) like to travel with an entourage. Nothing says "I am important!" like a gaggle of trailing associates. And there is some legiti-
macy to this—to a point. Playing a little theater is one thing, but
buying in to your own puffery is something else. Too much grandstanding will *cost* you credibility, and may even make you look like
a talking head instead of the boss—definitely not Alpha.

Arguably the best way to give yourself the confidence required
to be Alpha is to…*prepare.* And then prepare some more. Slavishly
obey Rule #3 ("Prepare; Then
Prepare Some More"), and prepare like your life depended on
it—because, frankly, your career
*does* depend on it. As I explained

> **Pro Tip:** Don't imagine them naked. Imagine them wrong.

in Rule #3, simply knowing your stuff is not enough—you have to
*know* that you know your stuff. And you must have confidence
that you truly, fully know your stuff. *That* is the confidence that
lays the foundation for being Alpha.

Moreover, preparation is not only a path to Alpha, it is a flat-
out requirement for *being* Alpha. "Alpha" is a strange blend that
requires both preparation and confidence. Without proper preparation you will not have the substance to back up your Alphaness.
Being Alpha is not just a front: To be Alpha is to be real. Without
the underlying substance you are not Alpha, but merely a blustering buffoon. Don't be a buffoon. Be Alpha. And to be Alpha you
*must* follow Rule #3. Prepare; then prepare some more.

## SHARE THE MAGIC

Much like credibility leaks upward, Alphaness leaks downward.
You, as the lead negotiator, gain credibility from having credible

experts, and in return you can apply your Alphaness to boost your expert. All too often, niche experts are not Alpha, and may perhaps even be quite timid. They can have all the credibility in the world, but without some Alpha to back it up they are no good as experts in a negotiation. That is where you come in. If you watch an experienced negotiator working with experts, you will see that the negotiator will not simply let the expert loose, but will guide the presentation, much like a trial lawyer questions an expert witness on the stand. He will interject common-speak explanations, ask clarifying questions, elicit credibility-boosting facts, and in general lend his Alphaness to the expert even as the expert lends her credibility to the lead. With skill and care, you can take that Alphaness granted by your team and share it right back.

Alpha is not a zero-sum game.

Team-based Alphaness is a dynamic creature. Even if you did enter the room carrying the partner's briefcase (not Alpha), your opponents will quickly notice if the partner turns to you every time a difficult issue comes up. If you speak boldly when called upon, your Alpha creds will increase quickly, along with your personal credibility. Similarly, if your team members routinely contradict or overrule you, then you are not Alpha and the opposition will stop treating you as Alpha.

There is generally one "lead" negotiator for each team. Having multiple people on the same side talking over one another leads to confusion and undermines the authority of everyone. It is therefore important, *before* any negotiation session, that the team understand who will take the lead during negotiations (I would suggest not using the term "Alpha" with your clients during these discussions). Failure to have a firm understanding of who will run the show from your side will make you *all* look bad.

A good team can create its own Alphaness. A bad team will destroy it.

Does that mean that there has to be an explicit statement of "Jim will take lead?" Not necessarily. Being that explicit can be good and useful, but sometimes it is not necessary to state out loud who will take the lead. When is it not necessary to state out loud?

Why, when there is a clear Alpha already established on your team, of course. Whoever is running the show during your internal conference calls is Alpha, and the presumption will be that this Alpha will be the front-person during the negotiation.

> At the proverbial 11th hour of a torturously long negotiation, one of the minor parties to the transaction (a government agency in a small country) decided to play holdout, and refused to sign the agreed-to documents. We put an iron-willed associate on a plane to meet with the Minister of Finance and other government officials.
>
> She returned the next day, signed documents in hand.
>
> According to witnesses, she spent half an hour in a room with the officials. She ordered them to sign, and simply stared at them until they did.

Team support is an important (and sometimes necessary) element of being Alpha, but it is not the only way to Alphaness. If for no other reason than that you will quite often be the only participant from your side, you need to be able to be Alpha without an entourage. You will be able if you learn how to be Alpha among a team of Alphas.

And even if you are the team Alpha, this is not enough. Being team Alpha is no guarantee that you will be Alpha enough to stand up to opposing counsel. And while being team Alpha is ego-boosting, that is not where score is kept. You need the confidence to stand up not only to your own teammates, but, more importantly, to the wolves on the other side of the conference room.

**Pro Tip:** Never throw a teammate to the sharks. He will drag you down with him.

Also remember that even when alone, you have a team. If you are alone at the negotiation table, that means that someone had enough confidence in you to appoint *you* the sole representative of the entire firm at this event. Supervisors? You don't need no stinkin' supervisors! The very *absence* of a team is all you—and your opponents—need to see to know what your team thinks of your abilities. Find strength where you can.

## TAKE WHAT IS YOURS

There will come a time, early in your legal career, when you enter a negotiation session, and your opponent is a man 35 years your senior. He is a senior partner at a prestigious firm. He has elegant gray hair and an expensive suit. Your boss, and your boss' boss, mention his name with reverie. In fact, they stopped by the meeting to shake his hand while ignoring you completely. This man was, quite literally, practicing law before you were born. He was Alpha while you were wetting your diapers. His résumé is a mile long, and he did more deals last month than you have so far in your entire career. He oozes credibility. He is slightly peeved to discover that he is negotiating with a rookie, and he does not suffer fools. *This* is your opponent. You look at him and realize: Playtime is now officially over.

   You will lay out your position, explain the facts and the law, and state your claim. And then he, this larger-than-life imposing figure of lawyerdom, will look you straight in the eye and simply declare that you are wrong. You. Are. Wrong. As the world stops turning and time stands still, you know that this is your moment of truth. Because your job, right here, right now, is to look him right back in the eye, and with equal confidence, without missing a beat, without a quiver in your voice, declare that no, in fact, you are right—and then prove it. To do this, to accomplish this feat of pure willpower, you must be prepared to

> **Pro Tip:** Everyone is wrong sometimes. An Alpha accepts this and is not rattled by a mistake.

the point of absolute confidence—knowing in your bones that you are, in fact and in law, correct—and you must possess the casual, almost arrogant confidence of a true Alpha.

These moments of quasi-melodramatic stare-downs occur with some regularity in negotiations. If you are so completely confident that you are right, so absolutely certain that the other guy is wrong, so unflinchingly sure that you know your stuff that you could stare all day long without blinking, if you truly are resting on bedrock of true confidence...*then* you will be Alpha. Then you *are* Alpha.

But don't wait for that staring contest. Use that bedrock confidence to shape your aura from the beginning. Let your knowledge of your own abilities wash over you and envelop you in impenetrable armor of steely-eyed comfort. Smile casually and let your opponent's weak attacks fall harmlessly away. Nothing can rattle you. Nothing can shake you. You are in charge.

You are ALPHA.

# Rule Number 15

## Break It Down

Negotiations are almost always complex. It is a rarity that there is a single issue, being negotiated along a single dimension, with a single, static goal. Real-life negotiations are not limited to canned facts and single issues such as we see in mock trials and debate tournaments, but instead consist of a mosaic of moving parts, some parts moving faster than others, some seeming to be more important and then disappearing to be replaced by other moving parts. There are a *lot* of things going on, and you have to keep track of it all.

This mosaic can be overwhelming to the rookie, and failure to address the complexity head-on will render you useless.

To manage this complexity, you must break it down.

This goes back to Rule #1 ("What Are You Trying To Achieve?") and Rule #2 ("What Are *They* Trying To Achieve?"): You start by identifying and breaking down the goals of each party, but you must go further. *Everything* must be broken down—current issues, potential issues, arguments, facts. They all interact, and you must track their current status, their potential future status, and the effects of their current and potential interactions. This sounds like a daunting task, for the same reason that the raw mosaic looks intimidating.

Once you get your hands dirty, however, you will discover that this is neither daunting nor intimidating—and it can be one of the most fulfilling parts of a negotiation. Like much in our professional lives, it is simply a matter of breaking it down, one piece at a time.

### Listmania!

Make a list. Make many lists. As you gain experience, parts of the process will become more of a mental exercise than anything else, but I would encourage beginners to write things down as much as possible. Even if you do not keep or use your notes, the simple process of writing down bullet-points will force your mind into structured thinking. Lists are an invaluable tool, and as a beginner you may want to surround yourself with written lists (it has been suggested to me that keeping written lists becomes important again for elder partners).

List out all the interested parties and their goals and cliffs. List out all the documents. List out all the issues. List out the positions of the parties on the issues, including past positions and predicted future positions. List out current logjams and likely future logjams. Just. List. It. All. Out.

At this point in your career, you cannot have too many lists.

> **Pro Tip:** A shoddy list is better than no list at all.

Experienced negotiators also make heavy use of written lists—when you go to the negotiation meeting, chances are fair that there will be a semi-formal agenda. Where do you think that agenda came from? In some form or other, we all use lists.

These lists force you into doing something important: thinking about one thing at a time. They force you to see the trees without getting distracted by the forest. It is all too easy for negotiators to fall into lazy mental habits. Mental laziness leads to weak arguments such as "there are many reasons why the price is too high." You are *pretty sure* the price is too high, and you *kind of*

> **Pro Tip:** The closing checklist is a good starting point for your issues list.

know why the price is too high, but you can't quite formulate it. This type of argument is a result of failing to organize the issues beforehand.

Don't let that be you.

So…break it down. Why, *exactly,* is the price too high? Take it one point at a time. Identify the point and consider it. Can the point be broken down further? What are its implications? Does this goal rely on other goals? Does this fact strengthen your position? Does this issue conflict with the previous issue?

> I worked regularly with a mid-level associate who was notorious for her meticulous list-keeping.
>
> I was watching her during a particular negotiation session, and realized that she was not merely taking notes—she was making lists. She was listing out the arguments and issues, matching them up, and listing out her planned responses along with the prepared compromise positions.
>
> She was doing this live during the meeting, not as a follow-up exercise. I suddenly understood how she was so quick to develop insightful responses to her opponents' arguments. Through her approach, each issue, argument, and counterargument was broken down into its component parts, ready for comprehension and immediate use.

Go about this task in an organized fashion. Do it by topic, by document, by feature, by party—even by color. I don't care. But do not just sit down and start listing out "important stuff in my deal." You are certain to miss something. Even the breaking down must be broken down.

## ONE IN A ROW

This just means you take one point at a time. Parse it out, break it down, then list it out.

It is a simple, iterative process—one step before the next—and unlike many other iterative processes this is not tedious. Rather the opposite, as this is the process that *immerses* you in the subject matter. Every point you list helps shape your strategy and makes the next point easier to grasp.

It may sound like I want you to spend hours listing out facts and issues, and sometimes you will do that—but usually not. This process can be fast. If you have a quick conference call to discuss a limited number of issues in a contract, it will take you only a few minutes to jot down the issues, note the contract sections that apply, sketch out your arguments, and note your compromise positions. Those ten minutes will put you in a position to respond to nearly anything your opponent says, instead of falling back on "there are many reasons why the price is too high."

Does this all sound a lot like Rule #3 ("Prepare; Then Prepare Some More")? Yes? Good.

This same approach applies to your analysis of the arguments you face. While applying Rule #6 ("Sit Down And Shut Up") and listening to your opponent, you should be writing down his arguments. You cannot respond to an argument you have forgotten.

Now having written the argument down, you must parse it out. Break the argument down into its component parts. What are the premises, what are the conclusions? Are there unstated premises? Which parts are just hyperbole and fluff? This is where you apply Rule #16

> **Pro Tip:** Margin notes in a contract are useful, but that is not a list.

("Logic Is Your Friend"): You will not be able to respond to the logical argument as a whole, but must penetrate the outer hull of presentation and look at the innards. Break it down.

## EXPLORE THE UNIVERSE

An essential tool for breaking down issues and arguments is the hypothetical. Ask yourself (or your client, or your opponent, as appropriate)...hypotheticals. Hypotheticals are wonderful exploratory tools, and will help you (and others) under-

> **Pro Tip:** Issues change. So should your lists.

stand how the different parts fit together. Hypotheticals allow you to theoretically change a single fact, thereby breaking it apart from everything else, which is the first step in breaking all the pieces apart from each other.

Having broken the argument down into its component parts, you will now be able to match up the component parts to your lists of issues, contract sections, and goals. You will not know how to respond to an argument if you do not understand the contractual origins (if these are contract negotiations) of the premises or the issue implications of the conclusion. *You cannot argue against a whole.* You must identify and evaluate each individual piece, separately.

When doing this you will also discover something else useful: You and your opponent actually agree on many things, and you will be able to identify those agreements. Agreements are just as important as disagreements, because agreements are things that you do *not* have to negotiate. Somehow people seem to find a way to spend (waste) lots of time negotiating points

> **Pro Tip:** Clients hate comma-induced stalemates. Really, really hate.

where they already agree. But by properly applying this Rule you will waste no time negotiating agreements, and will instead focus all your effort on negotiating genuine *dis*agreements.

Breaking down the issues and arguments—along with applying Rule #1 ("What Are You Trying To Achieve?") and Rule #2 ("What Are *They* Trying To Achieve?")—will also help you avoid the common problem of getting trapped in the contract. Most business negotiations involve a contract of some kind, and it is easy—especially with a room full of lawyers—to get stuck negotiating the words of the agreement instead of negotiating the *purpose* of the agreement. The words of the contract should reflect the agreement of the parties, not the other way around. By focusing on specific parts of the puzzle and the underlying goals, you can get past comma-induced stalemates.

The mental approach described in this Rule is central to your success. You simply cannot gain a full understanding of any subject matter unless you break it down. If you do not break it down, you will be unable to identify your goals (or theirs), you will be unable to gain understanding to the point of confidence, you will not be able to apply logic, and you will not be able to establish credibility. If you do not properly break down the issue, you will be doomed to rely primarily on hyperbole and vague generalities, and you will not have successful negotiations, or, at best, provide inferior service to your client. Either way you fail.

# Rule Number 16

## Logic Is Your Friend

We lawyers love hyperbole. We talk so much that we become good at it from sheer practice, and we can make almost anything sound good—or bad.

Hyperbole is fun, like a nifty parlor trick. But doing hyperbole well is also difficult to teach (or to learn), and it is not nearly as powerful and effective of a tool in negotiation as logic. And you had better believe that good negotiators are good at logic, whether or not they are also hyperbole-loving lawyers: Logic is the meat and potatoes of good negotiation. If hyperbole is the flash, logic is the substance. Structure an argument, state the premises clearly, state the path to the conclusion clearly, and state the conclusion most clearly of all.

**Pro Tip:** Logical analysis is easier when you write things down.

Chances are pretty good that whenever you see a negotiator engage in excessive hyperbole he is trying to cover up a shoddy argument. Hyperbole is the smoke and mirrors of argument. When you cannot tell what the premises are, or how they relate to the conclusions, your BS-detector should go into active-seek mode.

**Pro Tip:** …and sometimes easier still if you draw a picture. I keep a whiteboard in my office for this purpose.

Not only should you not be distracted by the hyperbole, but you should zoom in on it, because more likely than not that is where you will find the logical weakness. And the plan of attack you will use to penetrate the fog of hyperbole is simple:

1. Identify each premise.
2. Identify each conclusion.
3. Apply logic.
4. Win.

This does not mean that hyperbole is bad. You should learn (and use) hyperbole yourself. What you should not do, however, is use hyperbole in place of proper logical argument. Logic is your sword and your shield against blustering. An argument based in sound logic is kryptonite to hyperbole and grandstanding.

In public discourse it often seems that hyperbole defeats logic. And indeed this does happen—but only because logic requires time to present and time to consider, as well as an audience both willing and able to do so. Sadly, some or all of those criteria are absent in much of our lives. As a result, you will occasionally find yourself negotiating in a situation where logic cannot defeat hyperbole due to a lack of any of those requirements. When that happens, by all means go nuts with the hyperbole.

> I once attended a sales presentation for "vacation packages." Not surprisingly, the presentation was all flash. Snazzy graphics, pictures of happy vacationers, and promises of great savings.
>
> The hard facts were harder to come by. In the face-to-face sit-down after the group presentation I requested a simple cost break-down. Instead I got another sales pitch.
>
> After repeated insistence I was finally given the numbers and the actual contract. I then requested time to read the contract. The salesman assured me that I didn't need to read the contract, but eventually relented. I ignored his annoyance and proceeded with my due diligence.
>
> Now having the time to carefully examine the legal and financial terms of the proposed transaction, I was able to parse the numbers and determine the actual cost. This was not particularly difficult once I had what I needed. I was then able to make an informed decision on the merits.

But in most of the professional business negotiations that you will face, hyperbole alone will not win the day. Business negotiations are typically drawn-out affairs, and players on both sides want to have (and insist upon having) a thorough examination of the issues. This is not fertile ground for empty hyperbole.

This means that hyperbole alone is unlikely to succeed. You must grasp the logical implications of the issues and the arguments. This means that you must master logic, for without it you will not succeed. You cannot bluster your way past professional negotiators, which is what most lawyers are (and business leaders and government officials as well). Even if you can fool some of the people all of the time, you will be able to fool few professionals any of the time.

The bad news is that logic is difficult to teach or explain. The good news is that it is not rocket science, and it mainly requires disciplined thought. The study of formal logic is not required. What *is* required is the patience and determination to think each issue through. Don't let yourself get rushed by pressure, either external or self-imposed. Apply Rule #15 ("Break It Down") and break the issue down into its component parts. Take your time to carefully identify the causal relationships between the issues at hand.

Identify premises and conclusions in arguments made by opposing counsel. Evaluate each separately, and look for unfounded premises or unproven conclusions. Don't allow your opponent to commingle premises, or premises and conclusions. Don't allow conclusions to slide by on implication without identifying supporting premises. Look for alternate possible conclusions. And so forth.

Logic is step-by-step thinking. Don't skip or leap: One. Step. At. A. Time. No intuition allowed, no jumping past the "obvious" parts. Step by step—*every* step. That's really all there is to it.

Ask yourself hypotheticals. Go through series of "what ifs," taking each hypothetical through to its conclusion. What if your opponent is correct on this issue, what if you agree to this demand, what if the installation *is* legally a fixture? What if the facts are as claimed—does the conclusion follow? Examine every angle, real and theoretical. Be methodical and thorough. This is the same exercise discussed in Rule #15 ("Break It Down"), but this time it's for your internal use. This is no mistake: This Rule and Rule #15 go hand in hand, and neither Rule works without the other.

Breaking things down allows you to apply logic, and logic helps you break it down. Two sides of the same coin.

Everyone reading this book is smart enough to manage the logic required for business negotiations. Where people fail is not in the capacity for logic, but in the application of logic. Attorneys get rushed and sidetracked—by un-goals, by personal concerns, by insecurities, by impatient clients, by emotions, and by a dozen other things that get in the way of deliberate and impassionate consideration of the issues at hand. You can do this, if you allow yourself the time and just let yourself think it through. And— importantly—the same applies to your opponent. Your brilliant logic will do you no good if your opponent is too distracted himself to understand. Conversely, if you do need to go hyperbolic, use un- goals to put your opponent in a logic-free state of mind.

Logic is important. Obviously. But at the same time it is not accidental that this Rule appears late in the book, after a long series of non-logic Rules. Yes, logic is required for a successful negotiation—but you knew that before you picked up this book. In fact, logic is often given too *much* deference in pre-negotiation preparations. You will review your argument and you cannot see how anybody could possibly withstand your amazing logic. And you maybe right…if your logic gets an even-handed review. Which it often will not. Your logic will be evaluated in the context of rel- ative credibility, against a backdrop of a myriad of environmental variables, by opponents who may not be nearly as motivated as you to spend the time to parse your argument.

Yes, you absolutely must have a firm grasp on the logic underlying the exchanges. But to rely on logic alone would be, well, illogical.

# Rule Number 17

## Nail Down The Weasel

A classic tactic in any debate or negotiation is doing the Weasel. Lawyers love this tactic so much that countless lawyer jokes are spawned from our uncanny ability to Weasel our way out of any apparent logic jam.

### DANCE THE WEASEL DANCE

How does the Weasel work?

We all know it: Just keep changing your position. Not a lot, not so much that you contradict yourself, but just enough to get out of a trouble spot. You made a brilliant argument (you thought) in favor of your position, only to have that argument promptly and irreparably destroyed by opposing counsel. Do you surrender? Of course not—you just explain that the argument you made earlier was not important, and not the real reason why yours is the correct position anyway; there are other, more important arguments, such as $x$, $y$, and $z$.

Essentially, you rendered irrelevant the efforts of opposing counsel. He wasted his time defeating an argument that you were ready to abandon at the first sign of trouble. You just successfully deployed the Weasel.

There are many versions of the Weasel, and they all build on the same basic idea: don't stay in one place. Keep your position shifting, moving around as needed to avoid getting nailed. Change the subject. Toss out a dozen arguments at the same time, like rhetorical cluster-bombs. The Weasel is sometimes a planned strategy, and other times simply a defensive reaction to getting stuck and not wanting to surrender. No matter. Avoid and evade is the Weasel in action whether it is conscious or not.

Full-on Weaseling is obvious and somewhat embarrassing, but the Weasel can be (and usually is) deployed in more subtle form.

A small "clarification" of my position will render your argument moot, as well as if I had stood up and done the Weasel dance. A careful Weasel can be frustratingly effective, and even difficult to spot.

Excessive Weaseling is annoying to onlookers and opponents alike, however, and you will lose credibility if you use it too much. While we have come to tolerate the Weasel as standard operating procedure for elected officials, there are limits to how much Weasel we accept from professional negotiators.

The Weasel is commonplace in everyday life as well as in "professional" negotiations, and you must master its use for your own benefit. More important, however, is that you learn how to face it. Why? The Weasel is the companion of insufficient preparation. If you follow the first three Rules of this book you will have relatively few occasions to use the Weasel yourself, but you will have ample opportunity to see it in action. The good news is that the Weasel is (at least in theory) simple to defeat: You have to nail down the Weasel.

> **Pro Tip:** When Weaseling, stick to oral negotiations whenever possible.

## NOD, LISTEN — AND TAKE CAREFUL NOTES

The Weasel lives in the world of vague positions, multiple interpretations, and alternate realities.

It is difficult to argue against a vague position. It is difficult to contradict, it is difficult to ridicule, it is difficult to break down into its components pieces, and a vague position makes it difficult to spot logical flaws. While a vague argument may be a poor argument, it is almost certainly also a persistent argument—it just will not go away. Arguing in a Weasel environment is like punching at air.

> **Pro Tip:** ...and when Weasel-Nailing, email is your friend. A written record is the bane of the Weasel.

In order to properly dispose of a vague argument and nail down the Weasel, you must make the position not vague.

But before you can de-vague-ify the Weasel, you must understand what the Weasel is saying. Don't *think* you understand the point—make *sure* you understand the point. This, by the way, applies not just to intentional Weasel behavior, but to anything said or written by the other side. You must be sure that you actually understand the point being made. You cannot nail anything down if you were not paying attention.

Sound easy? Well, it isn't. There are un-goals standing between you and the real point. First is the un-goal of wanting to appear smart. Nobody likes asking for clarification—it is so much better to nod sagely instead. But ask you must. You cannot let your own confusion, however slight, get in your way. You are pretty sure you got the point? Not good enough. Get clarification. You have to be sure that you are sure.

Second is the un-goal of wanting to hear yourself speak. We have this amazing ability to interpret what we hear to make it fit what we want to say. You just want to get to the awesome point you are about to make. As a result, you hear whatever you need to hear to set up your pre-planned statement. Nothing will deter you from your plan, and that includes your opponent not actually saying what you thought he said. This un-goal is devious, and will make you think you are sure of your opponent's point when perhaps you are not. But you have to check yourself, and make sure that you respond to the point that was actually made, instead of the point you wanted to respond to.

> **Pro Tip:** Always have a Weasely fall-back position ready. Just in case.

Gaining understanding doesn't have to be some big embarrassing admission of failure. Asking for clarification is standard. You need not feel embarrassed. Innocent ignorance and curiosity is harmless. Everyone wants everyone to understand. As long as you do not ask for clarification every time you speak, little harm will come to you.

Does this sound familiar? It should. This is essentially Rule #15 ("Break It Down") in action. Breaking it down and Weasel-Nailing are companion skills, with Rule #16 ("Logic Is Your Friend") riding in the back seat. You cannot stop the Weasel without first breaking down the points, and breaking down the points places you in excellent position to launch your attack.

## HAMMERTIME

Now that you precisely understand your opponent's actual point, let the Weasel-Nailing begin. Take the conversation beyond mere clarification. Repeat your opponent's point back to her, restating as needed for specificity. The words *"precisely* understand" and *"actual* point" above are not filler; to nail a Weasel you must command both. Ask her to confirm that you got it right. Play dumb as needed—but playing dumb is not usually required. Saying "I'm sorry, I didn't understand that, please repeat it" makes you sound dense. Saying "I'm sorry, let me clarify this point" accomplishes the same task without portraying yourself as the slow one in the group.

If the argument is compound (as Weasel arguments often are), break it down and get confirmation for each individual point. If there are important words and phrases being used, zoom in on those and ask for a definition—a discussion of the merits of gun control will be difficult to de-Weasel unless there is a clear understanding of the meaning of the term "gun control". Don't tell him what "gun control" means—let *him* define it. If he comes up with a silly definition, you press for more specificity...but let him dig his own hole. Make him offer up a *specific* definition of "gun control" and, for greater specificity, "gun" and "control" and any other term that comes up—and then make him confirm your excruciatingly specific restatement of his argument regarding gun control.

Nail. Him. Down.

No more vagaries allowed. No more changing the subject. No more "clarifications" after the fact. When faced with a Weasel you get your clarifications *up front.* Freeze the pieces in place on the board. The Weasel requires moving pieces in order to work. So make the pieces stop moving.

It frankly does not matter what position you eventually get her committed to. The important part is that you get her committed to *something*. It doesn't have to be a major point. It doesn't even have to be a particularly important point. Just get *something*, no matter how small. Once she is committed you can address her position honestly. If you nailed her down to a specific point, no matter how tangential, you can build from that. Apply logic to the now-fixed point, and extrapolate other necessary conclusions. All points in a negotiation are related; locking down even a small point can be a big step toward locking down the larger issues.

Locking down the pieces is the first step in Weasel-Nailing. It is a good defensive play that can render the Weasel mostly harmless, and once you have locked down a sufficient number of pieces, you can prepare to take the fight to the Weasel. You can treat the rest of the session as the negotiation equivalent of a cross-examination.

---

After facing a frustrating Weasel in an extended negotiation session, extraordinary measures were in order.

The senior partner leading the negotiations had an associate write down everyone's position on each issue on posters that he taped to the walls—all in the interest of seeking compromise, of course.

As we proceeded through the negotiation, the walls became covered in taped-up posters, and the Weasel was neutralized.

---

Now that you have your opponent committed to specific points, you can—and should—hold her to those points. Call her on any subsequent contradictions. Your Weasel-Nailing creates a record, the functional equivalent of a deposition, that you can use to keep her honest (or to attack her credibility) for as long as you are discussing the issue. You can take your time dissecting her position. She cannot escape without significant credibility loss, and must instead defend her selected position until the bitter end.

Of course, this only works if you took careful notes of all the specifics to which you forced your opponent to agree. You did take careful notes, right?

An important sidebar: Regular Weasel-Nailing does not need to be confrontational. You can gently nudge the Weasel with reminders of stated positions and allow—subtly encourage—an ordered retreat or silent surrender. You do not need to (and ordinarily do not want to) make a public spectacle of nailing the Weasel. Create easy outs for your opponent—and relatively easy wins for your side.

## GO WEASEL-HUNTING

Sometimes, however, regular Weasel-Nailing does not suffice. Maybe you are facing a particularly skillful Weasel, who excels at coming up with seemingly endless alternative justifications for his position. You think you have him nailed, only to discover that there are still more alternate arguments to support his position.

Now you have to go further still. Now you have to commit him to a hypothetical. Hypotheticals are versatile tools—we have already used them to organize and understand. Now we use them for attack.

Offer up this "clarification" to help resolve the impasse: "My understanding is that you support the death penalty because of the deterrent effect—is that correct? Yes?" And then hit him with the innocent challenge: "So, then, if I can show that the death penalty has no deterrent effect, you will agree that there is no reason to have the death penalty, right?"

Now you are nailing the Weasel down not only to a set of current positions, but nailing him down to a future position. This approach is far more effective than disproving deterrence and then demanding concession on the death penalty. If you prove first and demand second, the Weasel simply "remembers" that he also supports the death penalty due to closure for victims, retributive justice, etc.

> I love saying "Let's be specific" during negotiations. It is innocuous and inoffensive, sounds eminently reasonable in almost any context, and allows me to mix and match Weasel-Nailing with simple goal exploration.
>
> I also incessantly pose hypotheticals, often in the context of "being specific" to (legitimately) help clarify an issue and help me understand. Of course, there's always the ulterior motive of Weasel-Nailing.
>
> Also, I use "Let's be specific" and hypotheticals frequently enough during negotiations that each additional use (such as when I suspect there's a Weasel at the table) raises no eyebrows, so when I start Nailing for real, the Weasel hardly ever sees it coming.

The challenge approach puts the Weasel on the spot. If he declines to commit to what appears to be the logical result of his stated position, he looks unreasonable and loses issue credibility. If he commits he is...committed. If he decides to add another argument to the mix, that's okay. Repeat the challenge, this time with "if I disprove both of these arguments...." This challenge approach is powerful. It is also confrontational. Be careful that you do not risk too much credibility of your own: If you are unable to conclusively disprove any of those arguments—you are absolutely certain after your preparation under Rule #3, correct?—it is *you* who loses in the exchange. This type of challenge is common in trials and debates, but much less so in business negotiations, and for good reason. Use caution.

This challenge approach also has the frequent side effect of prompting a pre-emptive Weasel backtrack. Your challenge can give the impression of being a set-up, and implies that you have some relevant evidence. The Weasel can smell the trap, and may back off his point before you even present your evidence (assuming you actually had any such evidence). All of a sudden deterrence isn't really all that important anyway, and it doesn't really matter whether the death penalty is effective deterrence. This allows you to declare deterrence a non-issue without even having to address it, and demand that your opponent now provide some other support for his position.

## NAIL YOURSELF

One final word on Weasel-Nailing: You can use this process on yourself to bolster your arguments. A statement such as "If it turns out that X is not the case, then yes, I will agree to your price" is effectively nailing yourself down. This will make a powerful impression. It is essentially a commitment strategy, as described in Rule #18 ("Give And Take...Or Not"). Intentionally and clearly committing to a specific set of facts or arguments is a strong statement of your reasonableness and confidence in those facts and arguments, and will add to your credibility.

Of course, if you turn out to be wrong it will cost you. A lot. Therefore, don't be wrong. So you should not do this unless you are very, *very* certain that you are correct. Which you will not be unless you fastidiously applied Rule #3 ("Prepare; Then Prepare Some More"). I hope you applied Rule #3.

Before even thinking about attempting to Nail the Weasel, or yourself, prepare. Then prepare some more.

# Rule Number 18

## Give And Take…Or Not

Negotiation is a process. "Process" means that things move and change. That is the whole point of negotiation—to change things to the point where you achieve your goals.

As part of this process, two things will happen: You will ask something from the other side, and the other side will ask something from you. And, of course, neither of you are willing to immediately grant the other party's requests. If it were otherwise there would be no need for negotiation.

That means that as part of the negotiation process there will be give and take. Perhaps surprisingly, neither giving nor taking comes easily to beginners.

As I have mentioned more than once, keeping your opponent from his goals is not your goal—it is an un-goal. This emphatically does *not* mean that you should automatically grant every request that does not conflict with your goals. Giving is an art, and should be done deliberately and with great care. Give too little and you lose credibility. Give too much and you lose leverage. Balance is crucial.

As with everything else in a negotiation, before giving (or not giving) you must always apply Rule #1 ("What Are You Trying To Achieve?"). What do you gain by giving, or by not giving? What do you gain (or lose) now? What do you gain (or lose) later? Is this a request that you can deny without losing credibility, or do you stand to gain credibility by granting it? Is the request coupled with an offer to grant something in return? If so, how valuable is the offer? How does this fit with your top-level goal? With your intermediate goals?

After applying Rule #1 ("What Are You Trying To Achieve?") you must then apply Rule #2 ("What Are *They* Trying To Achieve?"). How valuable is the request to the other side, and how does it fit into their overall goal structure?

This analysis applies not only to requests from your opponent, but to offers from your side as well. You should not always wait for the other side to ask for something—beat him to it, and offer up a package of your choosing. When making an offer, you should consider the value of the offer to both you and your opponent.

Giving is not a goal; it is a tool. More specifically, it is a currency with which you can buy your goals, or "take," if you will. It can be difficult to take without giving. Sometimes you will not be able to achieve your goals at all without giving; other times giving is simply the easiest and quickest way to take. Either way, there will be gives—but make sure you get to take what you need in return.

## IT'S ALL RELATIVE

The basic (and somewhat obvious) rule of giving and taking is "give small, take big," or "get more than you give." Assuming a zero-sum game (which is a bad assumption, but a useful starting point), you will come out ahead if you exchange every give for a more valuable take. The important part here is to apply Rule #2 ("What Are *They* Trying To Achieve?"): "Value" is determined just as much by your opponent as by you, and you must understand *their* valuation. Fortunately, value is *not* a zero-sum game. Everyone values things differently—sometimes very differently. This can be a very, very good thing for you, if you understand and use those differences.

Identify potential gives that are valuable to your opponent but not particularly valuable to you. These potential gives are potential gold—but also potential traps. If it is clear that something is valuable to your opponent but not to you, you will only appear petty and unreasonable if refuse to give. If, on the other hand, the issue appears more valuable to you than it really is, take note. This issue is now a valuable bargaining chip. Issues like this are at the center of giving small and taking big, and are not to be given, but *traded*. You will suffer no credibility loss for not surrendering, and you can trade it for something you value more. These issues are valuable cards. Play them carefully.

Connected with this relative-valuation approach is the application of what might be charitably called "information management," and somewhat less charitably called "truth management." Despite Rule #4 ("It's All About Credibility") and Rule #5 ("Take The High Road"), you are not obligated to be entirely forthright with your opponent, and you are certainly not obligated to volunteer the relative value you attach to issues. This extends further: If you can deceive your opponent about valuation without violating those Rules, you

> **Pro Tip:** Use truth management with great care. The potential harm to your credibility is significant.

affirmatively should. Put on a show of surprised indignation (or, with a good trade, reluctant surrender) when facing a request for something you value less than your opponent thinks you do. Car salesmen aren't the only ones who can sell undercoating and destination charges. Your challenge is to do so without harming your credibility in the process.

> An expert was brought into a negotiation to discuss a specific issue. The expert believed that we were right on the issue at hand, but the issue meant far more to the other side than it did to our side.
>
> Before entering the room, the expert was instructed by the partner to argue the case well, but not too hard, because it had already been decided by our side that we would eventually concede the issue.
>
> We didn't want to concede the issue too soon or too obviously, and we wanted to make sure that it came as a request from the other side. We also did not want to appear so committed to the issue that our eventual capitulation would diminish our credibility.

Information management is key to trading small for big. No one would knowingly trade big for small, so you must convince them that they are actually trading small for big as well. Part of this is clever hyperbole, but mostly it is information management. Keep your opponents fully informed about some of your goals, but keep other goals—or at least their value—tucked away. Actively running false flags is riskier and more difficult, but can be very much

> **Pro Tip:** Re-valuing your goals is one thing—convincing your client of the new valuation can be something else entirely.

worth the effort if done carefully.

Do not limit your information management to merely managing your opponent's perception of your goals. You should also try to manage your opponent's perception of *his* goals. Make his gives look small and his demands unreasonably large. This also is part hyperbole and part information management, and is an important part of giving small and taking big.

> I happened to overhear a telephone conversation between an associate and a customer service representative of a department store where she had purchased some clothing. She was apparently trying to return a purchase.
>
> I heard the associate tell the person on the phone: "I have the receipt, but some of the tags weren't on the dress when I bought it. I probably can't return the dress without all the tags, can I, huh?"
>
> Surprising nobody, the store representative agreed.
>
> I decided it was appropriate to discuss position presentation with the associate before asking her to negotiate anything on behalf of my clients.

Beyond smoothing the path to agreement by making your requests look small, you can—and should—smooth the path to agreement by making it easy for the other side to agree. You can do this simply through the actual process of agreeing. For instance, when discussing matters with low-level officials (or, sometimes, not-so-low-level officials too), avoid asking their opinion on anything...or asking them to *do* anything. For understandable reasons, bureaucrats often have a default setting—a mindset—of "No." Most any substantive question asked will get the default response…so don't ask substantive questions. Instead, feed them the result you want. Make it easy for them.

"Hello! Can you confirm my understanding that you accept applications by fax after hours" is better than "Do you accept after-hours faxes?" Make it so all they have to do is nod their head. Nodding their head is easy. Considering a substantive question and making a decision hard. Make it easy.

## TIE YOUR HANDS

Except sometimes you should make it hard.

Information management (or truth management) can be applied in reverse as well. If you can make it appear that you simply cannot agree to your opponent's demand, or that it would be bizarrely irrational to agree, then you can effectively take the issue off the table without giving anything at all.

The extreme form of this technique is full and irrevocable commitment. Instead of negotiating about whether you should launch the product line, just launch it and negotiate about terms after the fact. Any request that you not launch is now irrelevant (although you have exposed yourself to other risks, of course).

A more common (and safer) version is to blame a higher authority, taking the issue out of your hands entirely: "The board has authorized me to agree only to X." or "I understand your point, but the lenders will not agree." You can thus maintain your stance as the good guy, without surrendering. These approaches are still risky—the other side may simply walk or call your bluff (*was* it a bluff?), and there is potential for significant loss of credibility.

Once you have tied your hands, appeasement comes back into play. Since you now simply cannot agree to your opponent's demands, she is left with no choice but to either accept your crumbs or go for the nuclear option. You have essentially turned what might otherwise have been an even-handed negotiation into an appeasement scenario.

This requires care—brinksmanship of any kind can lead to the nuclear option, but this is a decision you must make. You can choose to continue "regular" negotiations, or you can choose to raise the stakes and play for keeps. But if you choose the commitment route, deploy appeasement mercilessly. Appease, appease, appease. Be her friend, be the magnanimous donor, all while giving up nothing of value and getting (or at least keeping) everything that you really want.

Credibility is essential for the success of these commitment strategies. Consider the car salesman who "suddenly" has to get approval from his manager for the final price, or the Best Buy checkout clerk who insists that she does not have the authority to negotiate the price of DVDs. They are both making essentially the same claim—that they lack the authority to agree to a specific

> **Pro Tip:** Commitment strategies only work if your opponent knows about your commitment, whether real or imaginary.

price—but we accept this without question from the checkout clerk and (hopefully) not from the car salesman. Why? Credibility. The checkout clerk's position is backed up by years of experience interacting with checkout clerks. We have been exposed to "deny, deny, deny" by checkout clerks for decades, and we now take it as given. Checkout clerks have credibility in this regard. Car salesmen? Not so much.

## BE A HARDASS

Giving is dangerous. Yes, you must give, and yes, you must compromise. But beware—compromise is a favorite disguise of the Salami. It is easy to give away the whole Salami while thinking that you are making clever trades of small for big. So watch yourself, and keep track. At regular intervals, take stock of the situation. Determine the *total* gives and takes compared to your starting point. It is easy to lose track of what you are giving when you are giving just a little at a time.

But give you must. Carefully and deliberately, to be sure, but give. Giving is essentially a requirement for taking.

Except when it is not.

Sometimes you specifically should not give. There are several circumstances in which giving is either not required, or an outright bad idea. If you are getting Salami'd you have to stop giving. If you have nothing left to give you must stop giving. If you have nothing the other side wants you must stop giving. Other times, you can avoid giving just because you can. The Salami is getting without giving. Use it.

Sometimes it's even better. Sometimes, you really do have all the power. Sometimes there simply is no reason for you to give anything at all. If the nuclear option is painful to the other side but not particularly troublesome to you...why agree to any concessions at all? Remember, your goal is to achieve your goals, and unless "being nice and reasonable" is an actual goal for some reason, I encourage you to smash your opponents with the iron fist of "No" whenever you have a complete power advantage.

---

I was negotiating an agreement with an electric utility. They were required by law to offer their services to us, but they had a fair amount of flexibility in terms. They also had no particular interest in the transaction.

My review of their agreement revealed a particular provision that was thoroughly unacceptable. During the negotiation meeting, I told opposing counsel that the provision was "completely lop-sided, extremely broad, out of market, and absolutely unreasonable."

He looked at me, smiled happily, and said "yes, indeed it is."

We moved on to the next issue.

---

Don't be afraid to say no, even to perfectly reasonable requests that will cost you little, when there is no upside to you. Do not feel that you have to be "fair." "Fair" is irrelevant. "Fair" is an ungoal—unless, of course, your Rule #1 analysis says it is an actual goal. Preserving your issue credibility is important, but this does not mean that you have to look out for the interests of your opponent.

> A partner was negotiating a stock purchase agreement in a corporate acquisition. He generally took a hard line during talks, and this day was no different.
>
> At one point opposing counsel appealed to his sense of fairness. The partner's response was blunt: "'Fair?' I don't even know what that means. I do know that I am not about to limit your environmental liability."
>
> Later the partner told me, referring to that exchange: "Well, I'm not here to make friends. I am here to get my client a good deal."

You might also consider not giving as an intentional strategy, even when you do not have all the power. When presenting your initial position on an issue, do you start with an offer that is favorable to you but fairly reasonable, with an eye to a compromise solution—or do you start with an offer that is overwhelmingly favorable to you, and on the verge of being completely unacceptable to the other side, with the intent of granting only minimal concessions?

There is no generally correct answer, of course, but the point is that taking a hard line is a legitimate choice. Brinksmanship—*i.e.,* forcing the negotiation right up against the nuclear option—can be risky, but the spoils are good. If you think your

> **Pro Tip:** Every little email is important. Selecting exactly the right words will control the tone and presentation, and will support your characterization of facts and claims.

opponent will end up with their back to the nuke eventually anyway, why bother appeasing them on their way there? Skip the preliminaries and just force the issue without giving anything up in the process.

If giving will not get you what you want, you should not give. Trading small for slightly less small does you no good. You have to trade small for BIG. Your goal is not to get what they are willing to give, but to get *what you want.*

# Rule Number 19

## Watch The Tide

Most negotiations start out tentative—the parties are feeling each other out, and trying to decide whether they even want to come to an agreement. At this stage it is by no means certain that the transaction will be finalized, the contract signed, or the sale closed.

### Hustle And Flow

At some point in every successful negotiation, however, a corner is turned and deal momentum sets in. When there is deal momentum, the parties are no longer mentally deciding "if" there will be a deal, but merely deciding how and on what terms. When the parties have essentially resigned themselves to the fact that a deal will be reached eventually, then you have deal momentum.

When there is deal momentum, the tone of the discussion changes. The parties are no longer adversaries, but partners. Collegiality increases, and direct challenges are reduced—appeals to the other party's sense of fairness might even become effective. When there is deal momentum, the default setting is that there *will* be a deal, and the default setting is that the remainder of issues will be resolved on "standard" terms. The negotiation range of the parties is effectively limited, and the band of allowable tactics narrowed. With deal momentum in place, it is difficult and unseemly to take a strong or extreme position—after all, we are all in this together, right? And to threaten the nuclear option, well that's just plain rude.

It will come as no surprise that deal momentum favors the appeaser. Deal momentum weakens the nuclear option, which is the main defense against appeasement. The sense of inevitability that deal momentum brings makes appeasement even more powerful than it already is—hey, since we all know you aren't going to go on strike anyway, why don't we just hammer out this agreement and be done with it?

> We were in the early stages of negotiating a power purchase agreement with a utility. The utility had made it quite clear that they had not committed to do the deal with us.
>
> This was a concern, as we needed this deal to succeed, and we had several controversial points on our agenda for the next negotiation session.
>
> At our pre-negotiation meeting, we determined that we would open the meeting with a discussion of the regulatory approvals, which would be a collaborative process.
>
> We did so, and after thirty minutes of shoulder-to-shoulder discussion with the utility of how to get the future contract approved, sufficient deal momentum was established. The utility did not bat an eye when we subsequently raised our controversial points, and the agreement was finalized and signed in record time.

With deal momentum in place, the friendly un-goals—being nice, pleasing your opponent—become pervasive and difficult to resist.

When deal momentum is absent, on the other hand, extreme positions, the nuclear option, direct credibility challenges, and adversarial language...they are easier to use, and they all gain power. "Fairness" is once again a foreign concept, and parties feel generally unrestrained in seeking what they want. Without deal momentum, the friendly un-goals are weakened but the adversarial un-goals—defeating your opponent, keeping her from her goals—gain strength. Be vigilant.

Deal momentum works on a feedback cycle. The same arguments that work better with deal momentum strengthen deal momentum. A friendly tone is more effective with deal momentum, and it in turn makes the parties more inclined to deal with each other, thereby increasing deal momentum. Conversely, the adversarial arguments that are powerful when deal momentum is weak or absent can further weaken deal momentum. Threatening the nuclear option works best without deal momentum, and it can prevent deal momentum from setting in—or destroy whatever deal momentum you had.

Deal momentum, or the lack thereof, sets the tone of the negotiation, and determines which positions and arguments are available to you and your opponent. You must be cognizant of these effects and use them to your advantage. More importantly, you should attempt to manage deal momentum itself to your advantage.

> **Pro Tip:** Have some "safe" topics prepared and ready, in case the conversation takes an unfriendly turn.

Determine whether deal momentum favors you, and then shape the momentum to your liking. How do you create, or destroy, deal momentum? You take advantage of the momentum feedback cycle.

You fear that you are being appeased? Deal momentum is your enemy. Increase the rhetoric, take some hard-line positions, maybe even throw in a subtle (or not-so-subtle) jab here or there, if needed. Refuse to agree to seemingly reasonable requests from the other side. Rule #4 ("It's All About Credibility") applies, of course, and you must manage your credibility as well as deal momentum—but don't restrain yourself because of "be nice" un-goals. Whatever it takes…but make sure that your opponent (and your own client) is completely clear that the nuke is alive, and you are in no way committed to the transaction.

> **Pro Tip:** Have some thorny topics prepared and ready, in case the conversation takes a friendly turn.

Worried that the other side is getting ready to walk? You need deal momentum—stat. Agree to something—anything—to keep them at the table. Do something "fair." Order a nice lunch. Change the subject to a less contentious part of the transaction. Find something to discuss that you know both parties will agree on.

Deal momentum is a strategic, long-term consideration, and you should take the long view. But deal momentum can also shift quickly occasionally, so you must monitor and manage it at all times.

## Don't Flub The Putt

The point when deal momentum is at its most powerful, and potentially most dangerous, is at the very end of the transaction. 'Twas the night before closing, and all through the offices…everyone is committed to signing the contract. He who dares raise a new issue or objection will face the combined wrath of the entire group.

Yet, inevitably, last-minute issues do arise. How you deal with these will to no small degree determine your success as a negotiator. As in any other contest, the endgame is the part of the negotiation where the weak will surrender the lead and the strong will seal their victory. Let me state this in no uncertain terms: *Vast damage is often done to otherwise excellent agreements in the last hours before contract execution.*

The pressure to *Just close!* can be immense. This pressure will be partly due to social un-goals (dinners, weekends, flights, etc.) and partly due to real-world considerations (filing deadlines, financing, participant schedules, etc.), but it will be there, and it can be overpowering. Many skilled negotiators have buckled to this pressure and made last-minute concessions that turned out to be disastrous. Last-minute concessions, almost by definition, are not fully thought out and poorly implemented. Remember Rule #1 ("What Are You Trying To Achieve?"), now more than ever. Tread very, very carefully when addressing last-minute issues, or you might destroy what you worked so hard to build.

Realize at a minimum that the same pressures that affect your side are also likely to affect their side. So don't give a last-minute concession without something of value in return. It's their deal too. Never is the threat of the nuclear option more powerful than in these waning hours, and requests for last-minute concessions are the Salami in action. Recognize this, and turn your opponent's Salami slice into an appeasement crumb instead.

Perhaps your most difficult job as an attorney and a negotiator will be, after having craftily created and managed deal momentum for the duration of the negotiation, to then resist that same deal momentum at the very end.

## Don't Go With The Flow

Distinguish between deal momentum and temporary advantage. Deal momentum usually changes slowly, due to…momentum. Advantage, on the other hand, can shift quickly.

You must watch the flow of the debate. Much like a fencing match, a negotiation session has a dynamic energy, and that dynamism can define who will be able to score—and when. Sometimes the parties are feeling each other out, but often one party is clearly attacking while the other is just doing its best to defend itself.

Use this. When the moment calls for it, you can make your opponent's demand look unreasonable, or their justification untenable. Did you just score a hit by proving that opposing counsel was wrong on a point of law? Or maybe you made a particularly eloquent argument supporting your position? If you see him falter, do not let him recover, but press the attack. Push him to cede the issue *now,* and the next issue as well, while his confidence and credibility are both weakened. This is also a perfect time to hit him with some credibility arguments, and perhaps recharacterize some goals while you are at it.

Conversely, recognize when *you* are on the defensive. Fine, you are embarrassed and flustered that your opponent just poked a logic hole in your argument—I get that. But *do not surrender,* at least not now. Stall, change the subject, call for a sidebar, deploy the Weasel, fire off chaff and flares, call an injury timeout…I don't care what you do, but this is *not* the time to agree to *anything.* Your opponent almost certainly has caused you to temporarily underestimate the value and strength of your position, and you need to clear your head and regroup. Mere "advantage" may appear ephemeral and unimportant compared to deal momentum, but it is no less powerful. Beware.

# Rule Number 20

## Think Sideways

Up until now I have focused on the basics. Fundamental strategies and approaches that will keep you from screwing up too badly. But if you are to be truly successful as a negotiator, you need to do better than merely not screwing up.

So far I have also mostly discussed how to get yours. How to give and take, how to achieve your goals, even at the expense of the other guy—perhaps specifically at the expense of the other guy.

### Everyone's A Winner

But negotiation is not a zero-sum game. There are exceptions, of course, such as when the only thing being negotiated is a dollar figure, but in the vast majority of negotiations there are multiple factors, multiple issues, multiple goals, multiple everything. This complexity spells opportunity for the creative player, and for the clever and enterprising negotiator.

If you do your job right, everyone wins.

"Compromise" doesn't mean that you split the baby. Baby-splitting just means everyone loses. True compromise means that you found a way to get everybody what they needed. "Win-win" is not just a buzz-phrase, but an essential concept in negotiation. A win-win situation should be one of your goals. You should seek to achieve not only your goals, but your opponents' goals as well.

That is the mark of a skilled negotiator.

Remember, your job is to pursue the goals, ignore the un-goals, and avoid the cliffs. Keeping the other guy from achieving his goals is not a goal—it is an un-goal. The same is true for your opponent. If he is reasonably capable, or if you help him along, he will not intentionally keep you from your goals. The best way to get to a deal is to make sure everyone gets what they want—or what they think they want—especially if what you both want is not in true opposition, as it often is not.

> I was attending a contract negotiation session which had bogged down over a particularly complicated financial covenant. The parties could not seem to find common ground in the covenant.
>
> After continued frustration, the partner who was lead negotiator for our side stood up and took a couple of steps back from the table, and said, "okay, everybody, let's all just step away from the contract for a bit. What are we really trying to do with this covenant?"
>
> He proceeded to lead a collective exploration of the parties' real needs, and identified a compromise solution...after scrapping the difficult provision completely and starting anew.

Sounds obvious, right? Well, it is. It can also be incredibly difficult to accomplish. If it were otherwise, there would be no need for negotiation. We are negotiating specifically because some of our goals conflict with some of their goals, and that makes the "obvious" win-win scenario hard to reach, and sometimes hard to see.

Put a different way, win-win scenarios are perhaps not really hard to reach, but *only* hard to see. If you can identify the win-win, then achieving the win-win will usually not be too difficult. Identifying the win-win is the challenge, and it is worthy of substantial effort.

## RUN THE SWEEP

How then, do we identify win-win results when goals conflict? Two parts:

First, go back to the beginning. The beginning of this book, that is. Rule #1 ("What Are You Trying To Achieve?") and Rule #2 ("What Are *They* Trying To Achieve?") are still the most important Rules. Go back and read them again, this time focusing in particular on the parts where I ask you to understand the "real" goals rather than the stated goals. Then apply that principle to the goals in your current negotiation. Come to really *understand* the goals, instead of merely identifying them. Understand the goals behind the goals, and contemplate alternate paths to achieve those goals. Identify which goals (yours and your opponent's) might actually be un-goals. Even actual goals can function as un-goals when they are incorrectly valued.

> I was negotiating a supply agreement, and we were stuck on warranty obligations. The buyer understandably wanted a strong warranty, and the seller (my client) wanted to limit warranties.
>
> My client's true concern, however, was not about warranties offered, but about gaps between warranties offered and warranties received in turn from our suppliers—and these warranties varied.
>
> Having re-characterized our goal, we were able to agree on an arrangement where our warranty to the buyer was related to the warranties received from our suppliers. In most cases the buyer ended up with a better warranty, and our gap risk was minimized.
>
> Win-win.

Separate the primary goals from the stepping-stone goals. Separate the must-have goals from the kind-of-want goals. Apply Rule #15 ("Break It Down") and Rule #16 ("Logic Is Your Friend"). Break down the goals and understand the relationships among them. See which goals depend on other goals, and which stand on their own. The win-win usually involves avoiding the troublesome intermediate goals, so make sure that you understand which goals are which.

Second, think sideways. This means that you get clever with the learning from our reevaluation of the parties' goals. You search for win-win scenarios, you look for synergies, you think outside the box, you take the 40,000-foot view, you try to change the paradigm. Apply every annoying corporate buzz-phrase you can think of.

Yes, really.

Think sideways. Don't try face the challenge head on. Don't run into your opponent's goals. Don't be linear. This process requires that you be open-minded and innovative, and look for ways for both parties to achieve their goals to an acceptable degree, or ways for the parties to redefine their goals to avoid or minimize the conflict or risks. Thinking sideways means that instead of butting heads with your opponent, instead of trying to convince her that you are right and she is wrong, instead of trying to impose your way on her by sheer force of will, instead of trying to take what is hers and make it yours—instead of all of those things, you look for an alternate route that gives both of you more what you each want. You do an end run on the conflict, and find the land of milk and honey.

> **Pro Tip:** Don't be afraid to throw ideas out there. The simple fact of trying to compromise will gain you credibility.

Notice I said you had to be open-minded? That means open-minded about your own goals as well as your opponent's goals. In fact, it is usually easier to think sideways with your own goals than the other side's. It is usually easier to convince your client to restructure their goals than it is to convince opposing counsel to convince *their* client to restructure their goals.

> **Pro Tip:** Sometimes the "alternate" route is actually the most direct and straightforward solution.

You have to be honest with yourself and with your client, and step back from the conflict. If you were a disinterested party, what would be the logical route to success? You will often find that if you can give your opponent exactly what they want, at little *real* cost to your own goals—it might turn out that your initial objections were based in un-goals instead.

The same goes for your opponent and her goals. Your opponent is as susceptible to mis-prioritizing as you are, and her un-goals are as tempting as yours. Sometimes this is to your advantage, and you will encourage her to keep chasing the un-goal—but other times it is not. Help your opponent past harmful un-goals and minor sub-goals that are obstructing the deal, show her how they really don't matter, and refocus her attention on the truly important issues.

And that takes us back, once again, to Rule #1 ("What Are You Trying To Achieve?") and Rule #2 ("What Are *They* Trying To Achieve?"). Most of the time, thinking sideways will require that one or more goals is reconsidered, restructured, or reprioritized, and it requires that you do this without simply surrendering (or demanding surrender of) a goal. Demanding surrender isn't thinking sideways; that's just playing chicken.

## RUN A TRICK PLAY

Sometimes—or perhaps most of the time—there is a third component to identifying the win-win: you have to deploy information management. You have to persuade your opponent that your sideways thinking in fact allows her to reach her goals. This might require you to recharacterize her goals, and convince her that her goals are not what she thought they were—even if your re-characterization is not entirely accurate, objectively speaking. If you can persuade your opponent that 90 days prepayment is not really that important to her, and this allows for a sideways solution that *is* helpful to her, then this is a worthwhile endeavor even if 90 days prepayment actually is objectively important.

**Pro Tip:** When thinking sideways, don't forget whose side you are on.

The point here is to not attack your opponent's main goal head on—it is difficult to persuade anybody that their central motivation is wrong—but instead to identify intermediate goals that are standing in your way, and then attack those intermediate goals instead, or look to supplant those intermediate goals with better ones (for you, that is). Look for the win-win, even if you have to recharacterize a goal or two to make it happen.

Sometimes your opponent never gets her goals straight, and spends the entire negotiation working with un-goals and intermediate goals. No matter. The win-win analysis relies heavily on Rule #2 ("What Are *They* Trying To Achieve?"), and it is her perception rather than reality that is important—or, more aptly, for this purpose perception *is* reality. Re-characterize as best you can, but ultimately you have to work within your opponent's worldview, whether it is right or wrong. Find a solution that everyone *thinks* achieves their goals, regardless of reality.

Honesty might be the best policy in school and elsewhere, but in negotiation, be careful. You must manage information, and manage it with purpose. Frankly, if you are always completely honest with your opponent, you are not likely to do well as a negotiator. On the other hand, if you are never honest with your opponent, you are also not likely to do well as a negotiator. This dilemma creates a risk for you, but also an opportunity.

Sideways thinking is an important skill, and one that requires true insight into your opponent's motivations as well as your own. You will only rarely be able to identify a win-win when the parties' central goals are at odds with each other, but thankfully this situation is relatively rare. Sometimes main goals do conflict directly— but most conflicts are between intermediate goals, or between a top goal and an intermediate goal, or even an un-goal.

This opens the possibility of sideways thinking by the insightful negotiator. Every negotiation logjam is an opportunity for you to shape the outcome to your liking. Keep your eye on the ball. Focus on the main goals—everything else is an obstacle or a tool.

# Rule Number 21

## Win!

The purpose of the entire exercise is to win. So how on Earth do we go about doing that?

To answer that, we must return (of course) to Rule #1 ("What Are You Trying To Achieve?").

Why Rule #1 again? Because this is how we define "victory." We cannot determine how to win if we do not know what it means *to* win. While it is possible to achieve your goals without knowing what they are, it is not possible to *know* that you have achieved your goals without knowing what they are.

The sweet visceral joy of knowing that you really stuck it to the other guy, that your brilliant rhetoric made him surrender his central goal—that is not winning. Winning is the quiet satisfaction of knowing that you got what you wanted, even if nobody else realizes it. Keep your eye on the ball. Winning is measured relative to *your goals*…nothing else.

Litigators have it easy. If the judge rules in your favor you have won. The winning process consists of convincing the judge and jury. But while a trial is a negotiation of sorts, most negotiations are not like trials. You don't have to simply convince a disinterested third party like a judge—any old chump can do that—you have to convince someone who has an actual stake in the matter, usually adverse to your own.

You are a negotiator: You have to convince your *opponent* that you are right and he is wrong, and that he should give you something that he wants to keep for himself.

Sometimes this can be done by actually persuading your opponent that your point of view is correct. But while truth and justice might play a part, more often the truest path to victory is through Rule #2 ("What Are *They* Trying To Achieve?"). You must understand your opponent's motivations—*all* of them. Not just the goals, but also the un-goals and cliffs. Perhaps *especially* the un-goals and cliffs.

Negotiation is a social exercise. You can place your opponent in a position where he must either agree with you or appear unreasonable, irrational, unfair, or downright silly. You are, essentially, forcing him to choose between ceding the point or going off a social cliff. You open your arms to their surrender, and you make the alternative extremely unattractive. Even while you are trying to make surrender appear easy and painless, the fear of going off the social cliff will be your main weapon. And to wield this weapon, you must understand the nature of your opponent's cliffs. Confuse your opponent about the issues, so that he will agree rather than appear ignorant. Bring unopposed experts to the table, so that your opponent cannot refuse without looking the fool.

Similarly, steer your opponent toward her un-goals. Distract her with shiny objects. Flattery will get you everywhere. Make her feel good about herself by agreeing to something unimportant. Let her think she snuck one by you. Convince her that an un-goal is actually a real goal of hers, while downplaying her true goals. Allow her to gain glory at your expense. Feed her vanity—the vanity of an attorney is a hungry beast.

Appease your opponent. The importance and effectiveness of appeasement stands repeating. Again. Appeasement, done correctly, allows your opponent to surrender with honor while assuring victory for you. Appease, appease, appease.

Undermine your opponent's motivation. Rob him of his conviction in his own position; sow doubt about the adequacy of his information; lead him toward indifference. Boost your own credibility and tower over him to where he cannot make himself argue his points against you.

Everything in this book is built on this foundational observation: negotiation is a social exercise. Likewise, everything in this book is here to help you take charge of that social exercise and shape the result you desire. Negotiation outcomes are not random. Someone is shaping those outcomes. Let that someone be you.

Being a successful negotiator does not require amazing intellect or the touch of the Blarney Stone. Instead it requires methodical preparation, dispassionate evaluation of the issues, and—most of all—the ability and willingness to observe and understand your surroundings and the human participants. There are no shortcuts, as much as we might wish there were. But this is good for you. This means that you can get there, if you simply make the effort.

Success is there for your taking. Take a deep breath, jump into the fray with both feet (well prepared, of course), and *win*.

Good luck.

# ACKNOWLEDGMENTS

More than *Jagged Rocks of Wisdom: Professional Advice for the New Attorney* or *Jagged Rocks of Wisdom—The Memo: Mastering the Legal Memorandum,* this book was a collaborative, group effort. This is my most ambitious writing project to date—various versions of this book have been in the works for almost a decade. The final result came to be only after substantial re-writes following input from many readers. I am therefore hesitant to thank individual people, as I am bound to forget even one, which would be one too many. Nevertheless, I shall give it a go, with apologies to the inevitable, inadvertent omissions.

The contributors (both knowing and unwitting) to this book include current and former colleagues, clients, and opponents, as well as friends and family. Most contributors were happy to help with only a little arm-twisting required. These contributors include, but are not limited to, the following (in reverse alphabetical order): the entire Tippmann Forum community, Steve Silverman, that guy at Skadden, Eric "Ric" Redman, Paul Spicer, Paul Bargren, Mary Ann Christopher, Marianne San Millan, Marcus Wood, Jim Tynion, Jeff Atkin, Jason and Anneliese Corcoran, Howard Susman, Henrik Lund (my father, himself an experienced negotiator), Heidi Storl, Harry Carlson, Greg Jenner, Gary Palm, select but unnamed Farkers, Evelyn Kim, Elizabeth Hanigan, David Quinby, Brian Nese, Bill Holmes, Bevets, Ben Thomas, Ayia, and my clients who over the years have entrusted me with their causes.

As before, special thanks go to Thane Messinger, who has shown time and again that a small publisher can be a family of its own. Thane makes every project a collaboration, and makes writing books so much more than just writing books. I look forward to many more years and publications to come working with Thane and The Fine Print Press.

Finally, I owe infinite thanks to my wife, without whom this book would be the least thing in my life not to have happened.

# ABOUT THE AUTHOR

Morten Lund is a partner with the law firm of Stoel Rives LLP, where he practices in renewable energy development and finance, and is hard at work saving the world, one solar panel at a time.

Born in Oslo, Norway, Lund attended Augustana College (the one in Rock Island), and Yale Law School. He lives in the outer reaches of San Diego, and his hobbies include working, parenting, trolling the internet, and not collecting stamps.

Previously, Lund was a partner at the law firm Foley & Lardner LLP, and is the author of two prior books in the *Jagged Rocks of Wisdom* series: *Jagged Rocks of Wisdom: Professional Advice for the New Attorney* and *Jagged Rocks of Wisdom—The Memo: Mastering the Legal Memorandum.*

# INDEX

# OTHER BOOKS

# FOR THE STUDENT

COLLEGE FAST TRACK: ESSENTIAL HABITS FOR LESS STRESS AND MORE
SUCCESS IN COLLEGE,
by Derrick Hibbard
ISBN: 978-1-888960-23-5, 123 pages,
US$12.95

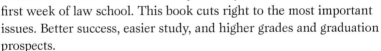

Concise, easy-to-read, and written in an
approachable, peer tone. Focuses on immediately usable habits to help in ways that provide
more—not less—time for enjoyment: success
*and* less stress. Once college begins, the reading load is heavy (and parties beckon). Thus "extra-curricular" reading is unappealing. *College Fast
Track* offers the *essential* habits for success in college.

LAW SCHOOL FAST TRACK: ESSENTIAL HABITS FOR LAW SCHOOL SUCCESS,
by Derrick Hibbard
ISBN: 978-1-888960-24-2, 93 pages,
US$12.95

For a law student, numerous and massive
assignments loom from the very first day—
with no let-up until final exams—and with
zero feedback until those finals. This book
focuses on the *essential* habits for your very
first week of law school. This book cuts right to the most important
issues. Better success, easier study, and higher grades and graduation
prospects.

LAW SCHOOL UNDERCOVER: A VETERAN PROFESSOR TELLS THE TRUTH
ABOUT ADMISSIONS, CLASSES, CASES, EXAMS, LAW REVIEW AND MORE,
by Professor "X"
ISBN 978-1-888960-15-0, 149 pages,
US$16.95

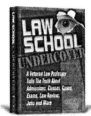

Written by a 20-year veteran law professor, this
book covers the most important aspects of law
school, from selecting the right law school to
admissions to first year to law review, moot
court, and though graduation and jobs. Offers
students the straight truth they will get nowhere else.

# FOR THE LAW STUDENT

LATER-IN-LIFE LAWYERS: TIPS FOR THE NON-TRADITIONAL LAW STUDENT,
by Charles Cooper
ISBN 978-1-888960-06-8, 288 pages,
US$18.95

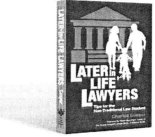

Law school is a scary place for any new
student. For an older ("non-traditional")
student, it can be intimidating as well
as ill-designed for the needs of a student
with children, mortgages, and the
like. Includes advice on families and
children; the LSAT, GPAs, application
process, and law school rankings for
non-traditional students; paying for law school; surviving first year;
non-academic hurdles; and the occasional skeleton in the non-
traditional closet. This book is a must-read for the law student who is
not going directly from college to law school...and offers an important
perspective for even traditional students going through 19 straight
years of education.

THE SLACKER'S GUIDE TO LAW SCHOOL: SUCCESS WITHOUT STRESS,
by Juan Doria
ISBN 978-1-888960-52-5, 162 pages,
US$16.95

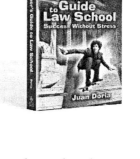

It is easy to fall into a trap of assuming
that one either strives and succeeds or
slacks and fails. Enjoying three years
of law school is not the opposite of
learning the law. There's also a tendency
to follow a herd mentality: the
assumption that there's just one right
way to do something, or just one way to
study the law. Too often, this involves too much make-work and too
much stress. This book will show you how to do law school right:
success without stress. (Or at least with *less* stress.)

# For the Law Student

LAW SCHOOL: GETTING IN, GETTING GOOD, GETTING THE GOLD,
by Thane Messinger
ISBN: 978-1-888960-80-8, 367 pages,
US$16.95

The key in successful law study is a minimum
of wasted effort and a maximum of results. Still
outlining cases? A waste of time. Failing to use
hypotheticals? A dangerous omission.
Preparing a huge outline? A dangerous waste
of time. Don't waste your time, and don't neglect what's truly
important. Learn law school techniques that work. Once you're in, Get
Good, and Get the Gold!


THE INSIDER'S GUIDE TO GETTING A BIG FIRM JOB: WHAT EVERY LAW
STUDENT SHOULD KNOW ABOUT INTERVIEWING,
by Erika M Finn and Jessica T. Olmon
ISBN-13 978-1-888960-14-3, 130 pages,
US$16.95

The competition for top jobs is intense, and the
special needs of law firm recruiters are
unknown to most law students. Most books
aimed at law students speak to how to get into
law school, and how to succeed in law school, but none address how to
get a lucrative job. This book is an insider's look at the secrets of landing a dream law firm job.


PLANET LAW SCHOOL II: WHAT YOU NEED TO KNOW (BEFORE YOU GO)—
BUT DIDN'T KNOW TO ASK...AND NO ONE ELSE WILL TELL YOU,
by Atticus Falcon
ISBN 978-1-888960-50-7, 858 pages, US$24.95

An encyclopedic reference. Examines hundreds
of sources, and offers in-depth advice on law
courses, materials, methods, study guides, professors, attitude, examsmanship, law review,
internships, research assistantships, clubs, clin-
ics, law jobs, dual degrees, advanced law
degrees, MBE, MPRE, bar review options, and the bar exam. Sets out
all that a law student must master to excel in law school.

# FOR THE NEW ATTORNEY

JAGGED ROCKS OF WISDOM: PROFESSIONAL ADVICE FOR THE NEW
ATTORNEY, by Morten Lund
ISBN: 978-1-888960-07-5, US$18.95

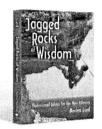

Written by a top partner, this no-nonsense
guide is a must-have for the new associate. Its
"21 Rules of Law Office Life" will help make
the difference to your success in the law: surviving your first years as an attorney, and
making partner. Beware. Avoid the dangers.
Read, read, and read again these 21 Rules of
Law Office Life.

JAGGED ROCKS OF WISDOM—THE MEMO: MASTERING THE LEGAL
MEMORANDUM, by Morten Lund
ISBN: 978-1-888960-08-6, US$18.95

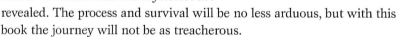

This book focuses on one of the most complex
aspects of professional work for a new attorney: researching, drafting, and refining the
legal memorandum. This book breaks the
process of the legal memorandum into "21
Rules." In these rules the mysteries are
revealed. The process and survival will be no less arduous, but with this
book the journey will not be as treacherous.

THE YOUNG LAWYER'S JUNGLE BOOK: A SURVIVAL GUIDE,
by Thane Messinger
ISBN 978-1-888960-19-1, US$18.95

A career guide for summer associates,
judicial clerks, and all new attorneys. Now in
its 14th year and second edition, hundreds of
sections with advice on law office life, advice
on law office life, including working with
senior attorneys, legal research and writing,
memos, contract drafting, mistakes, grammar, email, managing
workload, timesheets, annual reviews, teamwork, department, attitude,
perspective, working with clients (and dissatisfied clients), working
with office staff, using office tools, and yes, much more.

Recommended in the ABA's *Law Practice Management* and *The
Compleat Lawyer,* as well as in numerous state bar journals.